P9-CLW-798

Diane
Bless you!
Matt
8/16/16

Page 124

The Way Home

Stories from the Master

By Mathias Karayan

Drawings by Maria Monterey
Creative consult for book cover: Susanna Rose Manske
Layout by Barbara Campbell

Library of Congress Control Number:
2008907204

ISBN: 978-0-9820675-0-5

Also by
Mathias Karayan

Healing the Wound:
The Family's Journey through Chemical Dependency

For more information contact
Karayan Publishing
www.karayanpublishing.com
or
Karayan Publishing
P.O. Box 366
Buffalo, MN 55313

These books can *also* be purchased at:
BUFFALO BOOKS & COFFEE
6 Division St.
Buffalo, MN 55313
763-682-3147

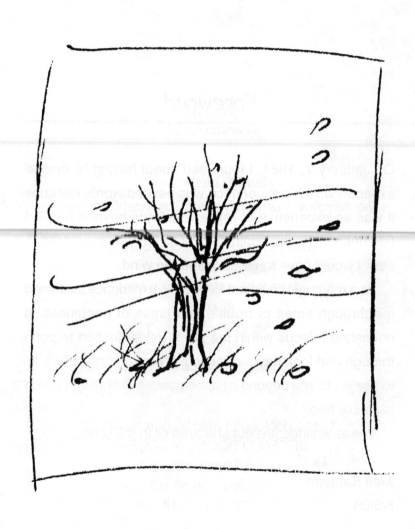

Foreword

On January 7, 1984, I journaled about having "a unique experience." This experience was beyond words because it was an experience of *joy,* a *revelation* beyond belief. I had been to the mountain. But it was not yet time for me to stay. I would have to go back into the wind.

As a memory I could not forget, this experience sustained me through times of trouble and times of happiness. It nourished a focus within me . . . a determination to push through and look beyond "all movement and noise" so as to see . . . to see beyond all appearances to only that which is plainly true.

These writings are but shadows of that journey.

Matt Karayan
8/8/08

Grateful Acknowledgements

To Lisa Hansen; who through her *many* proof readings consistently reminded me to keep the stories simple.

To my sister Maria Monterey; who reviewed the content through the eye of a hawk.

To my wife Rita; who provided the final touch of flow.

To Clelland Gilquist (Gil); who provided the opportunity for this project to come into fruition.

To Orton Tofte; who took the time and patience to listen.

To Barb Campbell; who through her creative eye brought pictures and words together.

To my teacher, through *A Course in Miracles*, my inner guide for direction.

Dedication

To my mother Magdalena,
Whose inspiration of unconditional love
Reminds me of The Way . . . Home

Contents

Introduction

Introduction

Along our way . . . and for awhile
    . . . our paths meet.

    Why we meet whom we meet
        . . . is a reason beyond us.
    It is a reason beyond why.
    A reason not yet ours to know.
    It is a reason beyond disappointment.
    It's ok to let it show.

    We meet each other to:
        Share
                Struggle
                        Support
                                & Grow

Beyond this is a reason not yet ours to know.

The only thing to remind each other,
        each and every day,
                is keep your mind, heart and soul
                    focused on The Way.

A Master Leads
by example,
not by words alone.

The Way

See joy in everything . . .

. . . and you see The Way.

Attend to laughter in all occasions . . .

. . . and you walk The Way.

Attract peace from every direction . . .

. . . and you *are* The Way.

The Secret Of
The Way

"Why do you speak in riddles?" inquired one. "Why not be direct?"

"Tales tell much to those who hear."

"You talk as if you have the answer," challenged another.

"I have no answer for anyone," responded the master with a mischievous grin, "least of all myself."

"And yet," added the master with a whisper, "in that lies the secret of The Way."

The Way To Move Mountains

"Master, what do you know about illusions?"

"Nothing," came the indifferent response.

"Well, I *am* surprised," said the cynic with a sarcastic, "gotcha" grin. "I thought a master knew everything."

Feeling mischievous, the master asked, "What is an illusion?"

The cynic was taken by surprise. Careful to word his response vaguely, he answered, "Well . . . it has something to do with responding to something that's not really there."

"In other words, an illusion is nothing?" surmised the master.

"I'll accept that," stated the cynic confidently.

"Allow me to rephrase your question then," directed the master. "What do you know about nothing?"

The
Silence
Of The Way

One day, the master was sitting with two disciples under a large oak tree. Two chickadees jumped about on the lower branches, chattering one to another, unconcerned with the three guests below. The three visitors watched the birds busily carry nest material to and fro. In and out of a hole above the visitors, the chickadees popped.

Stirring from his quiet contemplation, the master asked the two disciples (who were busy in conversation), "What are the chickadees doing?"

The first disciple replied in his usual wordy fashion, "The chickadees are obviously busy preparing for the cold winter by their hard, uninterrupted work of storing much food and building a secure nesting home."[1]

The master asked again, "What are the chickadees doing?"

The second disciple replied, "Bouncing to and fro with much chatter."

---

[1] Chickadees don't store food. And they certainly don't build nests for the winter—they build them in the spring for their eggs. In winter, they roost in dense conifer branches.

With a smile, the master leaned back against the tree trunk, lit a pipe and blew a smoke ring. "And what can one learn from the chickadees?"

The first disciple (who enjoyed any opportunity for giving long speeches to whoever would listen, or at least feigned to listen) stood up, gesturing ostentatiously as he spoke. "It is important to organize and plan for your future possibilities so when in times of need, you will find yourself with a secure plenty." Attempting to please the master, he added, "Then one might be in a position to help those less fortunate." For support, the disciple concluded with a quote, "As the wise ones of old would say: 'There is much virtue in productive hard work.'" Smugly satisfied, the disciple gracefully sat back down in his place next to the master.

Again, the master asked, "What can one learn from the chickadees?"

"Nothing more than what I've already said about their movements and chatter," stated the second disciple. "Why not?" responded the first disciple, feeling shown up by the second disciple's simple answer.

"I only stated what I saw," replied the second.

The first began defensively to say, "Well, I . . ."

"Shh!" interrupted the master quietly. "Listen." The moment was still. Even the chickadees had stopped their commotion. Finally, the master broke the silence with a whisper. "Anything beyond that is mindless chatter, nothing more."

Resting In The Way

Listen to the wind in the trees . . .

. . . It speaks of things to come.

Taste the water in the meadow brook . . .

. . . It remembers times past.

Watch the birds in the air . . .

. . . They tell of that which is.

Be there.[2]

---

[2]Anything and everything can be a metaphor to remind us of God's moment.

Allowing The Way

One day the master was found wandering among the briars beside a small brook. As he picked berries, a small number of students followed.

One student inquired, "Master, how is it that you can make no provisions for the comfort of your body? You seem quite unmindful of the conditions that exist around you."

The master stopped and picked up a nearby stone. "Take this stone," he said, putting it into the student's outstretched hand. "How does it feel?"

"It feels hard," replied the student mindfully.

"Use it," the master stated emphatically. The master then stepped down to the bank of the stream, motioning the students to follow. "Take your hand, put it in the stream. How does it feel?"

One student bent his knee. "It feels brisk and steady."

"Embrace it," the master said with feeling. Then he kicked off his sandals and, with a natural gracefulness, lightly walked through the stream. "Take your shoes off and touch the ground with your bare feet." Hesitantly, the students followed the master's directions. His smile encouraged their initial expressions of delight as their bare feet kissed the ground. Soon the entire group was dancing and laughing barefooted beside the stream as if there were no tomorrow.

Finally, the master concluded the festivity by motioning the students to gather 'round. "Now tell me," stated the master earnestly. "How does the earth feel?"

"It feels soft and warm!" one student observed.

"It feels ALIVE!" echoed the resounding response from all quarters of the surrounding hills.

"Allow it to flow through you,"[3] instructed the master.

"But, Master," the first student diligently asked again, "How is it that you can make no provisions for the comfort of your body? You seem quite unmindful of the conditions that exist around you."

---

[3]Beyond the conditions and distractions you *think* exist around you, is the Kingdom within you, waiting to be remembered. Therefore, anything can be a teaching aid for you to remember to allow the Kingdom to flow through you . . . when you *remember to* allow it to do so.

"When you allow—without resistance, without judgment—that which is around you, you experience being part of it, not being separate from it. I am unmindful of the conditions that exist around me because nothing exists around me." Then the master quickly and quietly picked up his sandals and skipped on.

Decision Along The Way

"Do I have to love everyone?" asked a frustrated disciple working at perfection.[4]

"You don't have to love anyone[5] if you don't want to," spoke the master, fussing with a briar bush that had snagged his garment.

"Huh?" came the confused response. "But I thought that . . ."

"To think you 'have to' do anything invites resistance," interrupted the master, releasing his hold on the offending branch in order to focus his attention on the student's question. "To 'not have to' decide anything frees your mind to listen. Those who do not hear their inner source's direction invite conflict because they do not trust their ability to freely choose The Way. Therefore, they feel they have to decide. And to 'have to' decide creates a pressure that invites conflict."

The master looked down again at his garment and chuckled. During his conversation with the student, the offending branch had released its hold and was no longer entangled in his clothing.

---

[4]What a wonderful phrase: "working at perfection"! As if it's something we attain by our own hard efforts! Just picture some Type-A, first-born overachiever thinking that if she just finds the right combination of behavior, she'll be perfect! The Way becomes clear when we *stop* working at it.

[5]You don't even have to like anyone. But that does not mean someone you do not like does not have a lesson for you to learn.

Truths Way

One day the master walked along The Way into town to mingle in the marketplace. A small band of disciples accompanied him. One of the disciples fell into an argument with an "outsider."

"How do you know there is any existence after the body dies!?" challenged the outsider. An argument that resolved nothing ensued. Finally, the master called the disciple over to ask about all the commotion.

The master patiently waited through the disciple's recitation of mindless details until she said, "I told him, 'There is no such thing as non-existence,' but he wouldn't listen to what . . ."

The master interrupted the disciple's discourse. "Why do you argue on behalf of a future state, unless you fear it? To be afraid is to block your journey to 'now.'

It is not in tomorrow that you find freedom from fear.

It is in the bird that sings its song.

It is in the wind that blows through the trees.

It is in the brook that bubbles along its merry way

. . . calling you to be free.

Let no thought of tomorrow stand in the way

. . . of your call to be free now.

Therefore, when you argue on behalf of truth, it is not truth you defend. Truth needs no defense!"

Hearing
The
Way

✳ ✳ ✳

As the master walked along a brook, a doubter spoke out a challenge, "Master, let's see you do a miracle!"

Without breaking his pace, the master responded, "If you want to sightsee, go to a circus. If you want vision, listen!"

Another skeptic continued the first one's heckling of the master, shouting across the brook, "Master—if you are a master—you should be able to tell me what I am thinking!"

Always enjoying an unexpected turn of words in any conversation, the master stopped and turned to say, "I'll tell you what you are thinking if you tell me how much change I have in my pocket!"

The skeptic scratched his head in confusion as the master walked on.

Change
Along
The Way

"Master," admonished a seeker, "*your* disciples should not have said and done those things!"

"Nothing in this world is mine,"[6] the master stated plainly.

"Even still," persisted the seeker, "they should not have done and said those things!"

"Try and change the world," the master responded.

"Master!" countered the seeker in frustration. "You exaggerate. I'm just talking about this one event!"

The master peered closely at the seeker. "What does trying to change this event and trying to change the world have in common?"

The seeker thought for a brief moment before answering. "I can't change either one of them?"

"Well answered," the master said approvingly. "Because you can't change this event, it might as well be the whole world."

---

[6]When you realize nothing is yours to own, the whole world becomes your playground.

Willingness
As The Way

One day, the master was sitting on a hillside giving a discourse on the enjoyment of all things without attachment to anything.

An aspirant from among the following multitude asked, "Master, you talk much about 'the joy of letting go.' How does one do such a 'simple thing,' as you call it? It has been hard for me!"

The crowd listened intently as the master softly replied, "The first step is so easy it requires nothing of you, just a little willingness."

"And what is this first step that easily requires nothing?" earnestly asked the one.

"It is the willingness to recognize that you do not know how to let go."

"But that's the problem!" the aspirant stammered with a frown that illustrated her frustration. "I don't know how to let go!"

"Listen!" whispered the master sharply. "That's not the problem; that's the answer. Because letting go has nothing to do with doing it your way, you can't know 'how to' because knowing 'how to' involves doing it your way. The real question is, are you 'willing to' without knowing 'how to'?

Walking The Way

"I think I'm ready," a seeker cautiously stated. "But I'm not ready to tackle the world!"

"No one is asking you to 'tackle the world.' Just take care to find *you*, and the world will tackle itself."

The Way Of Change

"Master, how many people need to be saved to change the world?" asked an inquisitive seeker.

"Just one," smiled the master.

"What are you saying?" asked the befuddled seeker.

"When you change the way you see your world, the world you see will change."

The Way It Is

See that lake? I own it.

But you can drink its water . . . if you want to.

See those trees? I own them.

But you can play in them . . . if you want to.

See the stars? I own all of them.

But you can look at them . . .
if you want to.

Today, I command
all Creation

To Be The Way
It Is.[7]

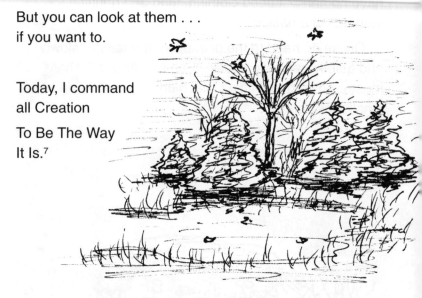

---

[7]True ownership is not possession as much as it is an understanding of right relationship. Because the master understands all nature to be a *substitute* for God's Kingdom (and therefore an illusion), he has no attachment to it and thus can freely play with the illusion. When you understand this, you can relax in the way things are and enjoy your "ownership" of all things.

The Perpetual Way

One day, the master was giving a discourse on the illusion of need.

Suddenly one from among the gathering crowd shouted back in an indignant tone, "What do you mean, I have no need? I need clothing, food and housing for starters—the basics!"

Giving no heed to the disruption, the master slowly and quietly began to speak. "See that flower?" The master pointed to a little violet hidden in the shade of a small rock nearby.

"I do!" snarled the annoyed one.

"Look at the color of its simple and unclothed beauty." The master looked back to catch the eyes of the annoyed one. Holding them in his gaze, he spoke, "*You* are that flower."

"Observe the flower's gentle strength," continued the master, looking to the violet. "It feeds from the ground of Mother Earth and bathes in the sun of Father Sky. You are that flower."

"Now look at the flower's unprotected freedom," emphasized the master, touching the earth with one hand and reaching for the sky with the other. "Mother is its foundation and Father is its cover. Wherever it goes, it is always at home. You are *that* flower." The master gestured to the crowd gathering around to see the flower and hear the master. "*All* of you are that flower."

The master sat back to relax against a tree, and spoke some more. The crowd pressed forward to listen, and this is what they heard. "Through intense heat and bitter cold, the little flower does not say, 'Why have you done this to me?' Through heavy rain and long drought, the little flower does not say, 'Why is your measure not balanced?' Through strong winds and damaging hail, the little flower does not say, 'Why do you not protect me?' For this little flower teaches daily the one lesson all need to learn. It teaches how to be. You will not find this flower complaining about how things 'should be' this way or 'should not be' that way, for it knows how to be. Its form one day will wither and die, but the spirit of the little flower never changes, remaining always within its perpetual beauty.[8]

You are that *flower*."

---

[8]Beyond the illusion of ever-changing appearances—You Are.

Insanity's Way

"Master, how do I make my life problem-free?"

"If you have a mouse that is a problem, get a cat! If you have a cat that is a problem, get a dog! If you have a dog that is a problem, get a leash! If the leash is not long enough, build a fence! Within a fence is a yard you have to mow. Get a lawnmower! A yard comes with a house. You will need a job to pay for it all! You will need to buy a car to get to your job to pay for your car! Is there no end?"

Trusting
The Way

"I think that everyone has to have something or someone to depend on. But I want to get to the place where I only depend on myself," said the disciple.

"It is best when you do not even need to depend on yourself," replied the master.

The Kingdom's Way

One day under the shade of an old oak tree, the master was teaching about the Kingdom of God. "The Kingdom of God is like a priceless jewel, realized as such when found. The finder sold *everything he* had to acquire this jewel."[9]

"Master," asked an inquisitive student, "where do I go to find this jewel?"

The master responded:

> *"If you listen for it, you might hear it in the wind*
>> *But it will elude your search.*
> *If you look for it, you might see it in a sunset*
>> *But it will elude your notice.*
> *If you feel for it, you might touch it in a hug*
>> *But it will elude your grasp.*
> *The Kingdom of God is not out there for you to find.*
>> *Choose again."*

"Master, please explain," the student asked. "I don't understand."

"God's Kingdom is everything that is eternal, never-changing. Look around you. What can you see that is never-changing?"

---

[9]Matthew 13: 45-46.

The disciples looked around and easily concluded that there was nothing around that was eternal.

"Then God's Kingdom must not be there," the master suggested. "And even though you work and worry to accumulate and secure your little kingdom as if it resides in the safety of a body, it will betray you in death. Either this is a cruel joke by God, or the Kingdom of God is not to be found there."

"Master, where is the Kingdom to be found?" asked the relentless student.

"The Kingdom of God is like an oasis in the middle of an endless desert. When found, the search for contentment is over."

Living
The Way

One morning the master took a walk into the woods. Along The Way, he found himself expounding on the virtues of enjoying all things in the moment.

A seeker from among the disciples asked, "Kind sir, how can I even begin to find time for a moment's rest when I am so busy planning my future to secure the essentials for my home and happiness?"

The master stopped to ask, "And where is your home that must be secured for happiness?"

"I live among the well-to-do,"[10] stated the seeker half-heartedly, "but I make no apologies for this. I have worked hard and long to secure this status."

"Are you happy?"

"I am working towards this," responded the seeker with honest sincerity, "but I admit to times of feeling disillusioned. That is why I have followed you to ask: Where does one find happiness?"

"Where I have been talking about?" responded the master with a mischievous grin. "In one's own home."

"But my home is not always a happy place," expressed the seeker, missing the point. "Where is this home of happiness you speak of?"

---

[10]Those who measure happiness as something tangible.

"Where does this tree live?" questioned the master, touching the bark of Old Mister Oak.

"Well . . . obviously right here," answered the seeker, confused about the direction of the conversation.

"Why?" pressed the master.

"Well, uh . . . I suppose because this is where it's at?" questioned the seeker, wondering when this conversation was going to have a point.

"And so, what about you, where are you now?"

The seeker paused to scratch his head. "Oh, I see . . . my home is where I am!"

"Well said, little one! Look at your roof of trees." The master stretched his arms upward and out. "How often does your roof need mending? Though it does leak," added the master with a laugh. "And your carpeted floor," continued the master sweeping his arms out wide. "How often does it need sweeping? What a relief to not have to do that!" chuckled the master.

"Oh, yeah, and all your numerous house

plants," added the master with a laugh while turning to look around, "Tell me, how often do they need to be watered?"

"Well, of course, never," responded the one with a laugh of his own.

"Isn't it amazing how your home knows how to be? Learn from it!"

The
Measure
Of The Way

One morning the master wandered along The Way into the city. The streets were buzzing with the hustle and bustle of a busy workday.

One of the numerous students who trailed along, following the master as he wove in and out among the sidewalk crowd, asked, "Master, why do so many work so hard, day in and day out, to acquire things and achieve status and yet never seem to attain any measure of lasting happiness?"

The master stopped among the jostling masses that were bent on accomplishing their forgettable errands. As the students gathered around, the master replied:

"There were three demons that came to earth and stole happiness.

The first demon said, 'I know where we can hide happiness so humankind will not find it. We'll hide it on the highest mountaintop.'

The other two demons laughed, saying, 'They'll find it there.'

The second demon said, 'I know where we can hide

happiness so humankind won't find it. We'll hide it in the deepest ocean.' The third demon laughed at both of them, saying, 'They'll find it there.'

The third demon said, 'I know where we can hide happiness and they won't find it until they look everywhere else. They will look into addictions of all sorts to find happiness. They will look into alcohol and drugs. They will look into gambling, sex, and eating. They will value above everything else the way they dress, the kind of people they associate with, what others think of them, the kind of job they have, the amount of money they make, the amount of things they accumulate, the look of their brand-new vehicle, but they will look here last.'"

"Guess where that demon hid happiness?" concluded the master.

"Inside of us," the student replied.

"As I said before," the master reminded,

"The Kingdom of God is within you.[11]

Yet, you do not believe it. And so it is that you will have to turn over every rock in your way in your search for peace of mind."

The noisy bustling crowd seemed to grow louder and larger as it continued to move around them like a series of

---

[11]Luke 17:21 (ASV)

great ocean waves, as though it wanted to wash them away. Those gathered around the master drew in even closer to protect themselves from all the jostling and to hear his words.

The master continued, "Your boulder field may be large, with many rocks to turn over. Or it may be small. You may have large boulders that require the help of others to move. You may try it alone, by yourself. Still the fact remains, you will keep turning over each rock until you recognize that all you find under these rocks in your search for peace is the deception of pleasure and pain. Then one day it will dawn on you that *truly* 'The Kingdom of God is within you.'

Those who do not remember this must search for and collect external measures. And yet all they find is pleasure and pain. What you look for outside of yourself as a measure for happiness is already inside of you waiting to be remembered."

The master looked around at the earnest faces encircling him. He knew that the many who heard and believed on one day fell prey to the world's pressure the next. Still, he continued to teach:

"Until then, it is the journey of many to continue to collect and add to their wealth as a means of gaining a happiness that continually eludes them. They do not know that the means they have chosen to find happiness is the very means that teaches them discontentment. For the world's measure of success as a means to happiness is also the measure of how far they have fallen short of their goal. And their goal? It is as fleeting as the dust in the wind.

This today and that tomorrow
But never the same as yesterday.

Therefore, many strive to collect and add pleasure and pain to their wealth of dust, all in the name of happiness."

"And beyond this?" asked a perceptive teacher.

"Not only is the Kingdom of God within you, but your journey through this seemingly body-based life experience has only been to remember that

You are the Kingdom that God created.

Any measure of lasting happiness will in the end come from this and this alone."

And they continued on . . . as if to disperse . . . into the crowd . . . weaving through the hustle and bustle of the city's so-called important affairs . . . unnoticed by all . . . who busily walked by.

The Way To Freedom

The place where you know you know nothing
Is your release to everything.[12]

"Then what's the answer?" asked the testy doubter.

"The only answer I have for you is the one you have already decided, for that is the only one you will hear."
"Arrgh, but how then do we get beyond our stubborn no-hearingness?"

"By admitting that your stubbornness in hearing only what you want to hear blocks your ability to hear your advocate for freedom."[13]

"And who is this advocate for freedom you speak of?" challenged the frustrated doubter.

"It is you . . . the real you beyond your raging ego," the master replied, quietly and gently. "And when you stop deciding how things should be,[14] you will be free to see . . . to see your creations unfold . . . through eyes of love."

The doubter stood, unable to speak, stunned by the love she felt flowing from the master's words.

---

[12]Loose translation from the Tao De Ching, # 71.

[13]The paradox is that when you recognize you are not a good listener, you put yourself in a position to listen.

[14]Although *thinking* was made out of a *belief* that you are separated from your Creator, the Spirit of Truth can use *your thoughts* to bring you back to your remembrance of knowing connection . . . *when you stop deciding how things should be.*

Choices
Along
The Way

"Master!" a seeker called out, trying to catch up to the master's brisk pace.

The master and all who followed slowed down to a stop as they came to a fork in the road. The seeker caught up, trying to catch her breath. "My, but you walk fast," jested the seeker.

"To stay ahead of the likes of you!" quipped the master in return.

"In all seriousness," started the seeker, "I have had many sleepless nights thinking of all the decisions I have to make."

"Why does this concern me?"

"Master," the seeker pleaded earnestly, "you seem to be at peace. How do you do it?"

"Do you want the shortcut?" asked the master with a smile.

"Yes, please," begged the seeker.

"Whenever you have doubt," directed the master, "know for sure without exception that it is between two illusions. Therefore, it does not matter which you choose."

"But how can you know that for sure?"

"Because if God wanted you to know, He would tell you. And because He has not told you, it doesn't matter."

"But I might do the wrong thing!" suggested the seeker nervously.

"The wrong thing is not in what you do," shot back the master, "but in how you perceive what you do."

"But that could be a justification for committing any sort of crime you want!" challenged the seeker.

"Which is only the justification of your right to continue your self-imposed sentence in your dream of hell."

"But some people's hell is not all that bad," the seeker stated, some uncertainty present in her voice.

"Not if your goal is peace of mind. You will always reap what you sow; the law of karma cannot be escaped except through love. And love's decision never makes a choice that would harm another."

"The Way you say it seems too simple,"[15] accused the seeker.

"Then I will give you the difficult version," laughed the master. The master gestured for all to sit as he started a story. "Once there was a grandfather who sat his grandson down to teach him about life:

'A fight is going on inside of me,' he told the boy. 'It's a terrible fight between two wolves. One is evil – he is

---

[15]The way you choose to see any situation is either the real problem that limits your ability to problem solve or the real solution (your miracle to freedom). It is that simple! *I did not say easy.* Therefore, when you change the way you see any particular situation, you will see clearly what it is you need to do.

lies, guilt and ego. The other is good – he is joy, peace, generosity, hope, empathy, humility, kindness, truth, compassion and love. This same fight is going on inside you – and inside all other people too.'

The grandson thought about it for a minute and then asked the grandfather, 'Which wolf will win?'

The grandfather simply replied, 'The one you feed.'[16]

The master rose, momentarily contemplated the fork in the road, then chose the path to the left . . .

. . . continuing briskly along The Way . . . unconcerned by his choice.

[16] A story from the Native American tradition

Playing Along
The Way

A disciple greeted the master gravely and earnestly, "How are things?"

"*Things* are the way I see them," the master responded, with a playful twinkle in his eye.

"Excuse me?" replied the confused disciple.

"Things are how you choose to see them. Nothing more and nothing less," the master stated plainly.

The Way Of Words

A follower, discouraged by all the words of deception he hears in his everyday life of relationships, approached the master and exclaimed loudly out of frustration, "Master, all I want is the truth!"

The master quietly offered the follower a comfortable place to sit, and began a story.

"Once upon a time, there was a cowboy riding along his merry way. Along The Way, his horse stumbled on a prairie-dog hole. Observing that his faithful companion had broken his leg and could go no further, the cowboy sorrowfully shot him in the head.

With the weight of the saddle and bags over his shoulder, the cowboy slowly trudged into the nearest town. In town he met a passerby who directed him to a stable that had a horse for sale.

"But the horse doesn't look good," the passerby added helpfully.

"I'll be the judge of that," returned the cowboy. "I've got a good eye for well-bred horses."

Shortly, the cowboy came to the stable and met an Indian who was selling the horse.

"The horse doesn't look good," stated the Indian. After looking the horse over, the cowboy could see that it was well bred.

"It looks fine to me," he said.

So the cowboy bought the horse, saddled up and rode out of town. Not far out of town, he found that his horse tended to meander into thick brush and deep ravines. Finally, and just barely in time to save his life, the cowboy jumped off his horse as it nearly trotted over a cliff. The cowboy stomped back into town and confronted the Indian.

"You sold me a blind horse!" the cowboy exclaimed angrily.

The Indian, shrugging his shoulders, replied, "I told you it didn't look good."[17]

The master looked at his discouraged follower and concluded, "What you make words mean to you is what they mean to you. Therefore, the deception you see starts with you!"

---

[17]A Native American story.

Way Beyond Belief

One day as the master spoke on the blessings of The Kingdom, a pious man from among the crowd started to quote sayings at the master about concepts of deserved punishment and hell.

The master easily shifted into one of his many stories about the Kingdom of God:

"Let us talk of a man who carries his precious treasure of gold with him wherever he goes. On his journey, he must carry his treasure in saddlebags on a horse through a turbulent stream. As he gets into the middle, the stream becomes deeper and more difficult to navigate. He cannot turn around, and yet, the weight of the treasure begins to pull the horse downstream. To save himself and his horse, the man could untie the treasure and let it fall away from them so that they could easily reach the other side. But the fear of the turbulent stream and his refusal to leave his precious treasure keeps the man stubbornly at his task. Another man on a horse comes by and offers assistance. The man stuck in the turbulence has an opportunity to hop on behind this other man and ride through. But the man refuses to abandon his treasure for the opportunity to ride out of harm's way. And so it is that this man is eventually swept away, treasure and all, to be seen no more."

"And what does this story have to do with what God demands of us?" challenged the pious man.

"The treasure of gold," continued the master frankly, "is the beliefs this man thinks can save him as he rides through the turbulent stream of life's dreams. Even though he has an opportunity to be free of the weight of beliefs and dreams that scare him, he holds on to them as if they will be his salvation. Even when he has an opportunity to see his beliefs from a different point of view, in the form of another man passing by to help him out of his dilemma, he refuses to give up his treasured fears and is swept away to die with them."

"How do you know which beliefs are of value and which ones are a hindrance?" asked a seeker from among the crowd.

"Because *all* beliefs are temporary, they do one of two things. They can keep you in bondage as cherished defenders of so-called truth, making all your choices limited by those beliefs. For example, if you cherish a concept of evil, you will limit your awareness to interpreting life experiences as being either good or evil. Because any other interpretation will threaten this cherished idol, you will see no other interpretation. You will remain stuck in a duality of good and evil."

The master continued. "However, let's say you are on a lifeboat alone, lost, drifting aimlessly on an empty sea of nothingness. Out of all of all the meaningless choices you think you have, only one choice has real merit."

"And what choice is that?" asked the seeker.

"Whether you want heaven or hell."

"But you talk as though heaven and hell are just metaphors!" challenged the pious man. "I believe they are real!"

"They are real metaphors," smiled the master. "Just like the life you think you live here. Any belief can be of value if it provides you with direction beyond itself towards your remembrance of a peace that is beyond belief. And that is the only value it has."

Too threatened by his interpretation of the master's words to take this opportunity to re-examine his cherished beliefs, the pious man went on the attack. "Who are you to speak as if you know what you are talking about? What you are saying sounds like a bunch of gobbledygook!"

"As you so chose to see it, so is it true for you. As I have said before, 'Be it done to you according to your faith.'"[18] Because the master could see the fearful anger in the man's eyes, he knew to speak no more and walked on.

When the disciples had time alone with the master, they asked, "Master, how come you were not offended by this man's inflexibility?"

"If I became angry with him for his beliefs, I would be no different from him. This is an opportunity to learn from him."

"How so?"

"Whenever you react to anyone, you are really reacting to your own beliefs. This is what you can learn from anyone who gets upset. Any belief you defend is a lie, because the truth needs no defense."

---

[18]Or belief. Matthew 9:29 and Matthew 8:13 (NASB)

God's Way

"Master, there are those that say there is no God. What should we say to them?"

"Be not concerned about those who practice beliefs different from your own. Rather be concerned that you still have beliefs to transcend. For every belief is a thought that is a barrier to knowing God. Just like everyone else, when you are ready to give up your cherished beliefs about nothingness, you will."

Prayer's Way

One day while the master was teaching on the power of prayer, one from amongst the crowd stepped up to ask, "Master, why is it that sometimes I get what I pray for, and sometimes I don't? Why does God seem inconsistent?"

"What do you think?" asked the master, turning to the attending disciples.

One disciple answered, "God doesn't always give us what we want because He knows what's best for us."

"Sometimes God gives us calamity to teach us a lesson," stated another disciple.

Another disciple answered, "God knows the attitude of our hearts and gives accordingly."

"Like God rewarding you for a job well done!" added another disciple.

"And," continued another disciple, piling platitude upon worn-out platitude, "God sees you as His worthy child. As has been said before, 'God does not make junk!'"

"But if you are God's children, as you say," challenged the master, "and Your Father who loves you more than anything else denies you nothing that you truly need, why do you need to ask for anything?"

To this question, no one gave an answer.

"Because your Father knows *you*, and not the dream for which you petition," continued the master, "think no more that prayer is about asking. Rather, start to use prayer as a means to commune with your Father who is the source of all gifts, and every gift that is for you will be yours to see."

"But," protested one fearfully bent on the need to ask, "we need to ask for what we need!"

The master responded in jest. "Has God abandoned His children? Does He withhold the inheritance He shares with you? Does He teach you through punishment? If this is so, it is a strange God you worship."

The master paused, hand held up to forestall protest. "Or is it perhaps better to understand that all that is yours to have is freely given when you are ready to receive it?"

The Way
Through
The Dream

"Master," asked an insightful student, "when you say that Our Father knows us but not the dream, are you saying that God has nothing to do with us in this world?"

"Again I will say, 'God does not know your dream of nothingness.' If he did, it would no longer be nothingness. God only knows you, His creation of Love. It is the Spirit of your memory of God, your right mind— rather than the father of all lies, your ego—which will lead you back to the remembrance of your Father . . . when you choose to listen. Therefore, ask away for whatever it is you want and make excuses for all the reasons why things happen the way they happen. And if it makes you feel better," quipped the master, "you could even say 'It was meant to be.' However, what happens, happens. It is not relevant. What *is* relevant is that you allow the Spirit of Truth, your right mind, to choose your meaning of 'what happens' to you. Commune with Your Father, who through your right mind will tell you everything you need to know so you can awaken from the dream you believe to be real."

Illusions In The Way

"Letting go is hard," expressed the troubled seeker.

"And is that belief not the greatest of all self-deceptions?"

"What do you mean?" came the startled response.

"Your struggle to let go is your witness to how hard you hold on to what you fear you will lose. But what you fear you can lose cannot be a part of you because you fear you can lose it! Therefore, your struggle is not in letting go. Your struggle is in your attempt to grasp and hold on to that which is not part of you. Can it be hard to let go of the wind? Only if you think it is yours to possess."

"But how do I know what is mine to have and not mine to have?" asked the seeker in confusion.

"When the body you seem to possess lies itself down for the final time, everything you can take with you is yours to possess," stated the master with a smile. "And because you cannot possess any person, place or thing, your struggles become opportunities to learn that you only let go of 'the illusion' of what you already do not have. You actually become more honest with yourself and therefore able to enjoy with gratitude all things that come your way. And you can truly enjoy them because you are not busy trying to grasp them."

"I'm still not sure I completely understand," stated the seeker in continued confusion.

"Be not the dog with the bone in its mouth seeing its own reflection in the water thinking 'that dog has a bigger bone than me. I want it!' Be the one to understand that to enjoy is not to possess. Therefore, teach no more the false idea that letting go is hard. For in truth, it is the easiest gift you can give yourself."

"And to hold on?" asked the inquisitive seeker.

"Is your impossible struggle," responded the master.

Mirrors
Along The Way

Confusion looks for its answer
in a cloudy pool.

The unsolvable problem seeks a solution
through the mind that imagined it.

Guilt looks for forgiveness
in a world of accusation.

Wisdom sees itself.

Confusion must be shown
that its pool reflects itself.

The unsolvable problem is gone
when the mind that imagined it is changed.

Guilt is forgiven
when truth is allowed to be its guide.

You are the cause of what you see,
And this you can change
when you choose to see it differently.

Surrendering
To The Way

One day the master was explaining that when one is ready to shake off the tyranny of time's hold on oneself, one will recognize that time is an illusion.

One of the young disciples expressed frustration, saying, "Master, when will all these things you teach be accomplished for me? I am sick and tired of living in my pain —I want out!"

The master calmly inquired, "Do you have patience?"

"I'm trying to," responded the disciple, with a feeling of hopelessness.

"Now listen!" challenged the master. "Your patience will get you there faster than your *trying* will."

"But, master," disputed a second disciple, "is not *trying* to let go a noble means toward leaving this world?"

"No!" returned the master sharply, to everyone's surprise. "*Trying* is a form of holding on to the world because . . . ," the master prompted the second student, ". . . *trying* is doing it whose way?"

The disciple paused in his thoughts for a short moment and then stammered in uncomfortable doubt, "Well . . . umm . . . uh . . . my way, I guess."

"And tell me," pressed the master, "do you know The Way to peace?"

"Well, umm . . . I think I have a pretty good idea," the disciple returned, feigning confidence amid his self-doubt.

"Then how do you account for your unhappiness?"

A cold sweat formed on the disciple's brow. He nervously stood with nothing to say (which was the smartest thing he had done that day).

"And you," said the master, directing his attention back to the first young disciple, "do you know The Way?"

"No, I do not," admitted the young woman.

"Now, listen, all of you. For what I say, all will learn in their own way and time."

The disciples gathered 'round the master in quiet anticipation. "You are right," reflected the master to the young disciple. "You are right in saying you do not know The Way to peace. For if you said you knew, you would have to account for your misery. Those who can account for misery's reasons are those who have found the means to peace. You are wise, young one, by stating that you do not know The Way. For those who think they know, and live not in peace, are the most miserable among humanity. And those who learn they do not know are not only students of The Way, but are also counted as wise among the ancients of old. For the words of The Sage handed down through time immemorial continues to speak to this generation, saying, 'Those counted as wise among the learned are those who know one thing more than the learned: They know they know not anything.' And in that realization is the road towards peace of mind, opened to you as you step out of your own way. Not only are you your own best friend, you are also your own worst enemy and therefore the only block to your peace. Remember, trying to reach for anything outside of your grasp is an opportunity for conflict. Letting go of that which is not yours to possess allows you to see what you already have. It asks for healing without condition."

"How do I stop fighting myself, master?" asked the young disciple, with tears in her eyes.

The master looked at this one with a loving gaze, recognizing that she asked unconditionally, with an open heart.

"Surrender to the battle without condition," he gently responded. "Let the cards of fortune fall to the wind. Cut the cords to the security you think you have and let the boat go adrift. Above all else, concern yourself not with the arrangement of the results. For the outcome belongs not to your hands alone!"

The dialogue ended. All sat before the master in contemplative silence as the sun set behind their shoulders.

Rays of light filtered through a cluster of brilliantly

colored purple, pink, and gray clouds. A central ray broke through to rest on and illuminate the master's face. As the evening sky faded to dusk behind the master, stars—as if reflected from the single ray— appeared in his eyes. Darkness raced across the sky as if to complete the appointed task of catching the last of the day. No one dared to interrupt this silence. It seemed sacred.

Letting Go
Of The Way

"Surrender—what is it, master?" asked the aspiring student.

"Let go of all you have learned, all semblance of wisdom, all thoughts of knowledge, all concepts of meaning and all projected agendas. Above all, give up the idea that you know how to surrender.[19] Then listen."

---

[19]That you think you *should* know how to surrender is a hidden form of doing it your way. The short cut is recognizing that you do not know how to surrender. That allows you room to listen to a message that is not of your own agenda.

The Way Of Repose

One morning, the master walked to the crown of a hill and sat under the shade of a large, lonely oak tree. The crowd gathered around the tree just below the edge of the hill's crown, settling in all the way down the hillside. They hoped to hear some words from the master.

That day, the master spoke on the virtue of the life of repose. "As has been said of old," stated the master, "'contend with no one and no one can contend with you.'"

One among the crowd stood up and faced the master to force a confrontation, to test him. "All well and good, you say, master," spoke this one boldly, "but what if you got robbed?"

The master stooped to the ground on one knee and crossed his arms on the other knee. While looking at the ground, he noticed a busy army of ants working on their little kingdom.

Finally, without looking up, the master stated quietly, "And if you owned nothing, what could they take?"

Unswerving in her defiance, this one maneuvered to avoid the answer by asking, "Well, then, what if they threatened to beat you until they took your breath away?!"[20]

The master continued his gaze on the little kingdom of busy ants. "And if you're not a body," asked the master calmly, "then what are you?"

"Why, spirit, of course!"

The master stood up and looked directly into her eyes. With a gentle smile, he asked, "Tell me, who can take that away from you?"

---

[20]An idiom for "breathed no more," or as we know it, "died."

Questions Along The Way

"Master, what's the greatest sin?"

"Fear."

"The best day?"

"Today."

"The greatest deceiver?"

"Self-deception."

"The most expensive indulgence?"

"Hate."

"The stupidest thing to do?"

"Find fault."

"The greatest troublemaker?"

"Talking too much."

"The best teacher?"

"The one who makes you want to learn."

"The meanest feeling?"

"Jealousy."

"The worst enemy?"

"Self-righteous anger."

"The greatest need?"

"Common sense."

"The best gift?"

"Forgiveness."

"Master, what if none of this is real?"

"It's not!"[21]

---

[21]Some excerpts are anonymous

Questions
In The Way

One of the students that followed along was constantly full of questions. "Master," he asked, "Where did the mountains, trees, rivers, sun, moon and the stars come from?"

The master replied with an entertained chuckle, "I'll tell you when you tell me, 'Where did that question come from?'"[22]

The student, not knowing how to answer, stepped back to ponder the question. He had no question to ask.

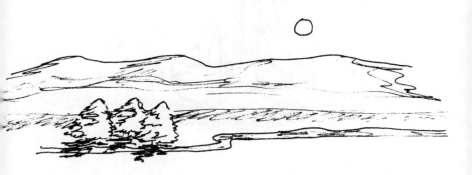

[22]A Buddhist saying.

Meditation's Way

As the master rose from a nap, he noticed a disciple sitting in a meditative position, with eyes closed.

The master walked over and playfully kicked the disciple's feet, asking, "What are you doing?"

Surprised by the interruption, the student looked up and responded, "Practicing."

"Practicing what?"

Hesitating to think, the student answered, "well, . . . practicing . . . uh . . . meditation."

"Meditation takes focus," reflected the master.

"I guess it does," responded the student mindfully.

"So do it well," chuckled the master.

The Way
Through Fear

"Master," questioned a diligent disciple, "you have said many times that 'There is nothing to fear.' Sometimes, it works to remember this when I find myself tempted to react to a situation.[23] Yet, there are times when no matter how hard or how many times I repeat these words, they won't get me out of my fearful thoughts. Why is this?"

"When you want your particular illusion[24] to be true, nothing you say will change your mind."

Looking for comfort in his illusion, the disciple continued by stating, "Master, sometimes I just want someone else to tell me that my fearful conflict is not true."

"The only one who can tell you that it's not true is the mind that made it real."

"And whose mind is that?" asked the diligent disciple.

"Yours," answered the master. "That is *why forgiving the way you see anything* is a gift you give yourself. Be patient, the results will follow."

---

[23]All temptation is the desire to make illusion true.

[24]*A particular illusion* is being specific about nothing.

The Way Of Release

One day, as the master walked along The Way, he taught on the virtue of acceptance and the snare of expectation.

A fearful comment was whispered close behind. "But you have to have expectations. It's just not realistic not to!"

Overhearing the comment, the master cut quickly to the heart. "Fearful one," spoke the master, turning around, "Your object of fear is not there. Nor does the world rise or fall by how you think things should or should not be. That you think you can control your own safety by having expectations is self-deception. For what you expect and what is real are two different things." With care, the master continued, "I promise you that the world will not fall apart if you release it from the grasp of all you expect."

Then the master leaned forward to speak compassionately to the fearful one. "The world you enslave with expectations always demands payment for what you expect! You will pay with disappointment, heartaches and tears. However, the world you release from your prison of expectations is a gentle world, giving you all you truly need for your healing."

The master turned to walk on. Pausing to look back, he smiled, stating, "Your little world of make-believe is what brings you your heartaches and tears. Release yourself!"

The Way
Through Nothing

One cool evening just after sunset, the disciples were fueling the campfire with wood.

A seeker quietly stole into the group unannounced, hoping for a private audience with the master. Anxiously, the seeker crept up to the large white pine just outside of the firelight, where he believed the master was resting. As the seeker approached the tree, it became apparent that the master was not there.

Suddenly, a voice from behind quietly asked, "What do you seek?"

Surprised by the voice, the seeker quickly jumped and turned. "Oh, you scared me!"

"You scared yourself," stated the master calmly. A student came to the scene to inquire about the commotion. The master assured her that everything was in order.

"Please, be seated," spoke the master cordially to the seeker, while finding a comfortable space himself between two large roots of the tree. The seeker sat down in front of the master.

"Kind sir," the young man started, wiping the sweat from his brow. "I seek you. For it has been said that you are a worker of miracles, a healer of minds."

"And what would you have me do that you cannot do?"

"Kind sir, I am plagued. I continually fear impending disaster. Nor can I sleep, thinking continually of tomorrow's fearful possibilities."

"Young one, look into my eyes." The master gently took the seeker's shaking hands into his own and gazed deeply into his eyes. For a quick moment, the seeker beheld a flicker of light in the master's eyes. Through the light came forth a place. Not a place in time, but rather an experience beyond space and time. It was an experience of being at peace. Oddly, this experience of peace felt as if . . . as if it belonged to him . . . as if it was his natural inheritance.

"Tell me, young one, do not all fearful possibilities fall into the category of 'what ifs'?"

As if to stir from a distant journey traveled before, yet seemingly close to his heart, the seeker slowly responded, "Well . . . I suppose they do."

"And tell me, young one, do 'what ifs' exist?"

"Well," hesitantly, "not really, but . . ."

So," interrupted the master, "when you worry about a 'what if,' what are you worrying about?"

"Well . . .," thinking out loud, "I suppose nothing, but . . ."

"Say it again," interrupted the master. "You are worrying about what?"

"Nothing," returned a cautious reply.

"Say it again," repeated the master with dramatic boldness.

"Nothing," responded the young one, more calmly and confidently.

"Scream it!" commanded the master's voice.

"Nothing!" shouted the young one, surprised by joy.

"Good, that's where you belong!"

"You know, I never thought about it that way."

"Start to!" directed the master. "Healing has come to you this day. For the miracle shows that 'anxiety's object' is always nothing.'"

Worry's Way

"You really don't have to worry."

"But it's impossible not to worry!" protested a cynic of The Way.

"I didn't say you *can't* worry," expressed the master clearly. "You can worry if you want to. I just said, 'You really don't *have* to worry.'"

Unreality's Way

"Master!" exclaimed an over-excited disciple. "Chastise that student. Though I know he is right about what he is saying, he keeps responding to whatever situation he is in by saying, 'It's not real!' He could be easily misunderstood by those who are uninformed about what we believe."

"That's his mantra," chuckled the master in response to the disciple's frenzy. "It's a nice way for him to remind himself, in whatever situation he finds himself, that words and behaviors mean nothing. It allows him to get out of the way, to be open to what the Spirit of Truth tells him. And if it means nothing to the mind that caused it, then it really is 'not real.' Maybe you should go up to him and tell him that what he is doing is 'not real'. He will probably agree with you."

The Way
To True Strength

One day, the master was found along a garden path lined with dancing flowers. Many others trailed along.

While the master was admiring the graceful flight of a hummingbird darting from flower to flower, an aspirant asked, "Kind sir, it has been said among the crowd that you are one who bestows great and wondrous gifts to those in need."

"And for what need do you seek fulfillment?" asked the master, keeping his gaze on the hummingbird.

"In my business, I have accumulated great wealth by my ability and shrewd management practices. But recently I have not only made some grave mistakes, but I have also inherited some blunders that have amounted to economic disaster for my business, colleagues and family."

"What have I to do with the daily matters of living that seem to plague humanity?" shrugged the master with indifference.

"I know these things are of no concern to you," expressed the aspirant, hoping the master would hear her through, "but I seek healing in my personal self-confidence." Dropping her head in shame, she continued softly, "For, because of this, I have lost all self-respect."

"Rely on the power of your own strength," remarked the master, watching the hummingbird dart from flower to flower.

In tears, she replied, "That is why I have come to you. I have no more strength. It has all been spent trying to correct my weaknesses."

The master released his gaze from the hummingbird and looked intently at the one. "And if you look only at overcoming your weaknesses, what will you see?"

"Weakness," she answered sadly. "I see weakness."

"And if you are looking at weakness," suggested the master, "will you see your strengths?"

The aspirant looked up and met the master's gentle smile in surprise and sudden understanding. Teary-eyed, she wiped her face and responded with more vigor, "No, I won't."

"It doesn't mean you have no strengths as much as it means you're just not looking in the right place."

Gifts Along The Way

One day, the master was found walking along a lakeshore. Many others trailed along.

While the master was admiring the graceful flight of a butterfly dancing freely with its own reflection on the water . . .one who was not a disciple but who had come to the master in distress earnestly asked, "Where do I look for what I need?"

The master, smiling with joy at the delightful butterfly, mused:

"Once upon a time there was a wise father who responded to his troubled son with a story.

'Son,' the father started, 'I once knew a young man who reminds me of you. This young man gave up everything he had to go to the jungle and capture a rare and beautiful butterfly. Through the heat of the jungle, he searched. In spite of mosquitoes and bugs, he searched. Through many torrential rainstorms without shelter, he searched. Lost for days in uncharted regions, he searched. At times he would catch sight of the butterfly from afar. Sometimes he got close enough to catch it. However, it somehow always eluded his grasp. Finally, after much time, energy and frustration, the young man collapsed under the shade of a tree. Exhausted by the chase, the young man bowed his head between his knees and cried. In defeat, he decided to give up the chase. Succumbing to despair and declaring himself a failure, the young man felt a soft touch. The butterfly had landed on his knee.'

Do you see the butterfly elusively skimming over the water?" asked the master, redirecting the woman's gaze.

"I do," stated the one in need. The group that followed along crowded around the master and watched the butterfly dance . . . as if it were dancing just for them.

"Tell me, why do you not look for the butterfly to be swimming in the water with the fish?"

"Master," answered the one with respect, "it is common sense to know that fish swim in the water and butterflies fly in the air."

"Then choose your common sense," emphasized the

master. "It will show you what your natural strengths are, should you choose to stop fighting them. A fish in the air has no more confidence than a bird in the water. And what is natural to you comes easily without conflict when you allow fear to rule you no more."

"And beyond this?" asked a teacher standing by.

"Beyond this?" reflected the master with a smile, "Beyond this, nothing else matters."

With all that said and done (lengthy discussions were tiring to the master), the master continued along the shore, enjoying the entertainment provided by the butterfly.

Vision's Way

Overlooking a hidden valley lost in the folds of a river bluff, the master stated in a fit of inspiration, "Creation's gentleness is all I see."

A cynic responded with disdain, "Some people worship creation rather than the creator."

The master gently added, "And others see evil in the world and respect neither."

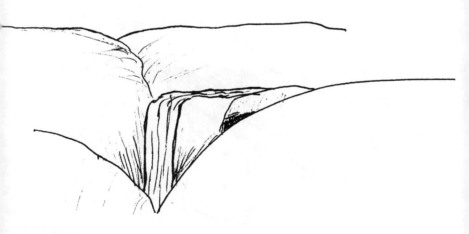

Wisdom's Way

"Oh damn!" stated a teacher in frustration, "I thought I knew all about _____ [25] only to find out I really don't. What a dummy I am."

"To know you do not know is not stupidity," spoke the master. "Rather, it's the first step to wisdom. As has been said of old, 'Know thyself' and the universe unfolds. And besides," added the master, "punishing yourself with words will not get you there any faster."

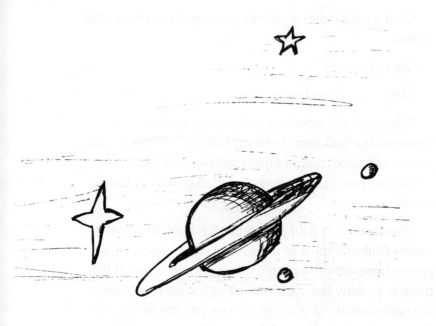

---

[25]Fill in the blank.

The Way To Peace

One day, the master was teaching on the virtue of peace from within.

A doubter rose from among the crowd and asked, "Master, I know you know much. But tell me, how can one find peace in a world full of hate, war and famine? How can one find peace in an ugly world?"

"And if one sees oneself as ugly," directed the master, "what kind of a world will one see?"

"An ugly world," the doubter quickly shot back.

"And what kind of world do you see?" continued the master.

"An ugly world."

"Why?" pressed the master.

"Well . . ." stammered the doubter, "I guess . . . because like you said, I see myself as . . ." The doubter swallowed hard, before finally saying, "...ugly." He wondered how this conversation had gotten all turned around.

"Think not that your peace comes from a peaceful world. Rather think that a peaceful world starts with peace from within. To confuse cause and effect at this point is to deny the source of all ugliness. For seeing ugliness outside of yourself makes you the world's victim. But your key to self-empowerment is realizing that the way your world seems to be is the way you choose to see it. Therefore, you cannot change the world, but you can change the way you see yourself and participate in a changed world. See the world of events as your means to peace so your healing may take its rightful place."[26]

---

[26]Why lament the world? Why try to change it, if it is true that it is merely the effect of your thinking? But to change your thoughts about it is to change the cause. The effects will follow.

Choosing
The Way

Without exception

Everything presented to you either reflects your conflict

Or an opportunity for you to accept peace

Within the midst of your conflict

You choose

Ripples Along
The Way

One sunny day, the master walked beside a calm lake. The disciples followed along, playing with and teasing each other.

One very serious disciple, thinking there was too much time spent in mindless bantering and play rather than on the importance of salvation, asked, "Master, what is it we are to learn as we walk The Way?"

"Only the opportunities that The Way provides for you to learn," answered the master simply.

"How will those opportunities present themselves?"

"As conflicts to your peace," spoke the master directly.

"Please explain," another disciple asked. Many others nodded in agreement.

The master stopped. He recognized he was going to have to present the long version. Behind him, the shore stretched out and small wavelets danced around his feet.

"Although certain situations present themselves as 'conflicts' to your peace of mind, they are actually opportunities to practice forgiving your perceptions of every person, place and event. As you begin to more consistently remember times when you found release from your situations of conflict because you changed your perceptions about them, you will see a cause-and-effect pattern emerge. You will begin to admit that your perceptions have not always been *unchangeable truth* as much as they have been justifications to defend a point of view that breeds conflict."

The master looked from face to face, nodding. "Now you are beginning to question your thinking like you never did before. Your usual way of thinking has not always been your friend. You thought it was a messenger of truth, but it deceived you. Your recurring conflict and your need to defend certain beliefs bear witness to this. But now you have started to realize that open-mindedness begins by seeing all beliefs as changeable and therefore open to re-interpretation."

"Master," asked a disciple who had seated herself on a log at the master's feet, "you say we have 'started' and we have 'begun' to act differently. How will we know when we have finally learned the proper way to respond to conflict?"

The master smiled at this one, who felt his love deeply, and responded, "Finally you will come to the place where you ask, 'How can I start to change my perception sooner to avoid the delay of extended conflict?' What at one time seemed obscure will now be seen as a shortcut. You will recognize that every conflict is a messenger, reminding you of your erroneous perception. And you will know when you have perceived erroneously because you will be in conflict."

The master picked up a rock and dropped it into the lake. "Ker-plunk," sounded the rock. Everyone watched as ripples quietly and effortlessly moved away from its center.

"Your thoughts are the only cause of ripples in the world," continued the master. "Therefore, real change only occurs at the level of your mind. You can decide where to drop the rock or what size the rock should be or what kind of rock it should be. But trying to change or fix the rock by focusing on the ripples is an absolutely fruitless endeavor that results in depression, frustration, anger and anxious fear. Confusing effect with cause is the source of all your problems. That is why *'The only function meaningful in time is forgiveness.'* True forgiveness recognizes that real change only occurs at the level of the mind and that the level of effect is merely the ripple of a world made real by the mind that thought it."

The
Seriousness
Of The Way

"Master," asked an attentive seeker, "how do I stay focused on the need to forgive my perceptions? My mind is so easily distracted by many different things!"

"What you thought was your enemy, you make your friend. Again as I have said, let your conflicts remind you of your need to forgive. You can use your conflicts as opportunities to practice forgiveness."

"But how can I forgive those who are zealous and pushy with an agenda of self-righteous beliefs that are designed to 'save' me or condemn me?"

"It matters not how others will perceive you; they have their own journey of personally empowered symbols to work through. What matters is that you remember you are practicing forgiveness for the consistency of your own peace of mind. Every zealot is a zealot in their own thinking, for it is your thoughts that charge your symbols with meaning. Remember, *you never react to anything outside of yourself, but rather you react to your perception of it*. So forgive your perception of the reactive zealot you see, because that is your brother teaching you that the reactive zealot is you. Be not deceived by what you think is outside of you. You always react to your own interpretation of anything. You are either the victim of or the savior of your own thinking. That is why *forgiveness is always a gift you give to yourself!* Everyone you meet is your brother and sister because they are the opportunities that remind you of this. In short, you learn forgiveness by practicing it. And to reinforce consistency of practice, you will teach it. Thus is it true, *we all teach what we need to learn."*

"So those who seem to irritate us the most are our best teachers for peace?" questioned the attentive seeker.

"Well stated," expressed the master admiringly. "Now, take one step more," suggested the master, to entice curiosity.

"What is that 'one step more'?" several disciples chorused.

"Allowing for no exception to rob you of your peace," responded the master. "No longer see anyone as a hypocrite, because it is you whom you condemn. You teach whatever it is you teach because you want to learn it. You want to learn it because you are not consistent at it. Like everybody else, you fall short of your words. That's why you teach it. The hypocrite, as you perceive him, is one who says one thing and does another. When you perceive another as a hypocrite, you see in him the inconsistency you refuse to perceive in yourself. That hypocrite becomes your savior because he becomes your opportunity to forgive the condemnation you refuse to see that you are doing to yourself. Forgiveness cancels out the duality by changing your perception. It reminds you that we are either all hypocrites worthy of punishment or we are all innocents teaching what we need to learn. Examine what it is you are teaching. Is it forgiveness or is it condemnation? For that is what you will be trying to learn. Examine what it is you are trying to learn. Is it forgiveness or is it condemnation? For that will be what you are teaching. Undo the world of nothingness by forgiving your judgment of it. In this way do you escape from your self-inflicted loop."

"Master," inquired the serious disciple, "all this you say, I do, and do diligently."

"Do one thing more," challenged the master.

"And what is that?" asked the serious disciple.

"Forgive your perception of how you see salvation as so serious, so you can play with your world of thoughts."

Playing With
The Way

A disciple asked, "Master, what about those who will resist this message of freedom from the world of thought?"

"As I have said," reiterated the master, who enjoyed playing with concepts, "though you can drop a pebble into a calm lake, you have no control as to where the ripple goes, or what it does." The master picked up a handful of smooth, flat rocks and started skipping them along the water's surface. Several disciples followed his lead.

But one seeker sat, lost in many thoughts. "Again, master," she asked, "please clarify?"

"Teach your truth through love, and when you allow your conflicts to remind you, forgive your perceptions that block love's awareness. Over this you have control. But what your lesson means to someone else is not for you to control or decide. Therefore, it is none of your concern. Your concern is to practice your forgiveness lessons, to undo your world of thought, and as you walk along your

Way . . . "paused the master with a smile," "you can have fun doing it!"

The master, seemingly mindless of the seriousness of salvation, continued to skip rocks in competition with the others to see who could create the most skips with a single throw.

Simplicity's Way

One evening, the master had just finished a discourse on the blessings of simple thinking. He addressed inquiries from the crowd.

A doubter, wishing to entrap the master in vain speculations, stepped forward and asked with feigned sincerity, "Master, if a tree falls in the woods and no one is there to hear it, does it make a noise?"

"It doesn't matter."

"Why not?" pressed the doubter.

"Because you're not there to hear it."

Irritated by his inability to nail the master down, the doubter carelessly pressed on. "But what if I was there?"

"Then you would know the answer to your question."

In The Way

One day, the master
decided to take a walk into
the city. A small group of
disciples and seekers
followed along. All of a
sudden and unannounced,
the master decided to stop
and rest his feet. In itself,
this was no problem. But he
sat down on the front steps
of the city hall courthouse . . .
in the midst of all the hustle
and bustle.

As the small attending
caravan gathered 'round,
one from among them
admonished the master,
saying, "Master, you can't
rest here, not in the middle of
all this business. You'll be in
everyone's way!"

The master laughed.
Then, as usual, he used the
situation as an opportunity to
teach on the virtue of being
in the world, yet not of the
world . . . while resting on the

busy steps of City Hall. Numerous questions arose.

"But, master," asked a curious seeker, "What about our responsibility for social reform?"

"Manipulating externals brings external change," stated the master, rubbing the bottom of his sore foot. "It is in the heart of each one that true reform begins."

Another questioned, "But, master, is not social reform necessary to aid in world peace?"

Recognizing that one's commitment to her comment, the master replied, "Then work in the world you still must do. For you yet need the world to bring you back to You!"

Not wanting to understand the master's words, a frustrated zealot stepped up to set the master straight. "What about issues of justice, the rights of those who are taken advantage of and oppressed! And those who live in poverty! Who will speak for them? And what about all the other humanitarian efforts going on 'round the world where wisdom is needed to help in their fulfillment for the betterment of all humankind?"

The zealot backed off to speak in a gesture of appeal. "My dear sir, I appeal to your common sense. Would you who are counted as wise among wisdom seekers not aid in the resolution of the world's problems? You among all others could be most helpful."

"Your words are sincere," stated the master gently, "yet they tremble with a troubled heart." Then, unexpectedly, the master's tone hardened to that of one intending to set a nail in place with one solid blow of the hammer. "The world is made of problems, just like problems make the world. Peace belongs to itself. Where the world resides, peace does not abide. Where peace abides, the world may not enter. Therefore, what belongs to the world must solve its own problems."

Unwilling to let go of her agenda, the zealot spoke with reckless anger, exposing her heart's fear. "If more people had an apathetic attitude like you, the world would be in chaos!"

"My dear one," smiled the master, "The world is chaos.[27] And you are provided the opportunity daily to step out into the light of peace, the place where chaos does not reside. True peace is absolutely changeless, while the world of forms is one thing one day and another thing the next day. Do you not know, can you not hear, are your eyes too blurred to see that the peaceful live in peace with themselves and thus with the world? While those in turmoil must live with the conflict of chasing the ever-changing shadows of forms in search of a consistency[28] that cannot be found! The conflict that lives within you presents itself to the world! This is why I say that those who live in the world need to solve the world's problems . . . because the world's problems belong to them!"

"But, master," expressed a troubled seeker, "it seems

---

[27]As a cause that comes not of God, chaos is mindless and aimless. Therefore, it would have no meaningful effect.

[28]Justice, meaning.

a bit selfish to ignore the world's problems, like you're turning your back on the suffering in the world."

"Those who look for peace within the chaos of the world are those who justify conflict as a means to peace. For to seek peace in a place where it cannot be found is the source of all personal conflict. All wars are personal projections of conflict justified in the name of securing 'self-righteous peace.' It is always a battle involving the denial of a conflict of interest!"

"However," continued the master, "to seek peace from within *yourself* is to forgive. Not to forgive chaos—chaos is chaos; what's to forgive? Seeking peace from within yourself cancels your own projection into chaos by forgiving *your perception* of it. A forgiveness that cancels out your projections makes you a natural part of the solution. Less and less do you react to your worldview when your diligence to forgive shows you a world that is meaningless. For who, when they see it for what it is, in the light of forgiveness, would react to nothingness?

"In the beginning, it is hard to forgive, because of your investment in nothingness. In the end, it is the easiest thing you can do when you see it as nothing to forgive. God will never ask you to do that which is already done. By forgiving your perception, you begin to realize that all you were trying to do was make chaos into a meaningful experience. Yes, there were some happy times, but there were also some sad, angry and fearful times. But now, as you walk along your Way, you can practice forgiving all your perceptions and still do all the good works you want without investing value in the outcome. Now are you truly part of the solution rather than a 'self-righteous reactor.' And remember," added the master, "it is not your responsibility to try to save anyone but yourself. Each will be ready to save themselves from their own 'self-righteous' worldview when they, in their own way and time, are willing."

"So relax!" summarized the master, sweeping his arms out before him. "Get out of the way! Practicing this kind of forgiveness is the only way to peace. The accomplishment of this task without exception is your final lesson."

The master finished resting his legs. The discussion ended. A number from among the group dispersed into the hustle and bustle . . . as if to be absorbed . . . by the world.

The Way Through

One day while talking to a crowd about the joy of uninterrupted peace, the master could see hopelessness on the faces of many. "Be true to yourself," encouraged the master, "and you will not have to leave the world. The world will leave you."

"But, master," questioned an aspirant in despair, "there are so many distractions, temptations and heartaches that the world presents. Sometimes I feel overwhelmed!"

"Young one, be of good cheer. Because your mind is powerful enough to create the experience of a world untrue to God's Kingdom, it is also powerful enough to undo it. Therefore, just do your part by practicing the lessons of forgiveness that The Way provides each day."

The Way Through The Ego

One morning, the master was wandering along The Way in uninterrupted peace. A passerby on his way to work unexpectedly crossed the master's path.

Taking this opportunity to resolve a question pressing on his mind, he asked, "Master, what would be a good and noble job as a way to further the cause of peace?"

"You can get involved in all kinds of social causes for peace or you can go to the mountaintop for peace," shrugged the master indifferently. Then his voice firmed. "But no matter where you go or what you do, you cannot escape your unconscious guilt[29] . . . until you undo it."

"How do I undo what I don't know is there because it is unconscious to me?"

The passerby's thoughtful response appealed to the master. "Through the level of thought and experience you recognize as having right now, you can forgive your perception of all people, things and events. This changes your perceptions as you remember them to be, as they

_____

[29]Guilt was made by you when you thought you left God. Unconscious guilt is unconscious because you have projected it on some unsuspecting form so as to avoid the condemnation of yourself you think occurred when you thought you left God. How clever the ego is.

are now happening and as you think they may be. I did not say forgive other people and events," emphasized the master, "I said forgive *your perception* of the other because it is your perception that forgives and condemns the world of form that you mistakenly took for real. Therefore, forgiving your perception is what brings you into the work of your own salvation."

The master emphasized his final point. "You see . . . you need to forgive your perception of *them* because they really are you, disguised by the ego as a body outside of yourself.[30] The Spirit of God will do the rest."

As the master turned to walk his way, the passerby hurried to keep the master's attention. "And what is 'the rest' that the Spirit of God will do?"

"This you do not need to know," stated the master. "Just do your part and the rest will be undone for you!" The master continued on in uninterrupted peace.

---

[30]You are the brother and sister that you see, seemingly made and projected as an individual by a separate thought of guilt.

The Unforgiven Way

"Master, what about the unforgivable sin?"[31]

"Because God has never condemned, He sees no sin to forgive. Therefore, the only unforgivable sin is the one you refuse to forgive."

---

[31]This statement has been the subject of much theological questioning. Matthew 12:32, Mark 3:29, Luke 12:10.

Knowing The Way

Before you thought . . . you knew.

Once you started thinking you forgot . . . what you knew.

Now you must use your thinking to remember . . .

    what you already know.

So you can think . . . no more.

But this involves a willingness to want to know . . .

    beyond thought.

And when this is all you want . . . you will know.

The Way To Hell

The master was in one of his jesting moods and asked, "When did Hell[32] enter God's creation?"

One of the disciples answered carefully, "Master, from all the things you taught us, it hasn't."

"Then let me ask you this," stated the master playfully. "What exists outside of the Will of God?"

"Nothing!" responded an attentive disciple.

"Nor does Hell," added the master.

"But, master," challenged a skeptic, "who's to say you're right?"

"If your investment in the belief 'there is a Hell' brings you peace of mind, by all means have it—it's yours. But know this, you will manifest what you believe, and your manifestation will reflect back at you to say, 'Look here, I'm real.' You will believe your manifestation to be your witness of hell's reality, not recognizing that your belief created it. And as you wait for the so-called 'unjust' to have their proper due, you will wait in hell."

---

[32]Hell as a place requires a capital letter. Hell as a concept, maybe not so much.

Freedom's Way

The master asked, "Is it freedom to do your own will?"

"It can't be," responded a fearful seeker. "My ego will roam to rule. I need to keep it under control."

"Your need to keep your own will under control is the ego's rule!" stated the master." Thank God that the ego's will is not your will. Not only are you the creation of God's Will, you are the Will of God. That is why it is freedom to do your will. It is through the wisdom of knowing the Will of God that you will know your will."

The Way
Through Flesh
And Blood

"Master?" questioned a skeptic, attempting to ensnare the master in debate. "There is much discussion about evolution and how we came about." As the skeptic began a lengthy discourse to define all the encamped positions of debate—atheistic evolution, theistic evolution, scientific evolution, intelligent design, creationism, etc.— the master found a comfortable seat for the ride. Finally, the skeptic wound down, saying, "Master, what do you believe about how we came about?" All mouths closed and ears opened to listen.

The master stood up and simply asked, "What does flesh and blood have to do with the Kingdom of God?"[33] And he walked on.

---

[33]Generalize: What does God have to do with any argument you have with another?

The Wonder Of The Way

In the heat of a day the master reclined under the shade of a tree.

He was finishing a discourse to the multitude on the peace that passes all understanding. A woman approached the master by pushing through the crowd. When she arrived at his feet, the woman, out of respect, bent on one knee with head bowed.

"Master," she started softly, "all that I own I give to you for this peace you talk about."

With gentleness, the master replied, "Woman, look into my eyes."

Half reluctant, yet deeply moved, the woman slowly looked up and met the eyes of the master. So sparkling clear, deeply mesmerizing, and appealingly gentle were the master's eyes that she allowed herself passage. Instantly she found herself as if immersed . . . bathing in radiant warmth of release beyond her troubled heart. "A release forgotten," she thought, "and how natural."

"What is it that you own?" asked the master.

Stirring from an instant in eternity, she answered "Just this." Stepping gracefully forward off her knee, the woman presented a shoulder bag full of various items, and food enough for her lunch. "Oh," almost forgetting, as she sank back onto her knee, "and these simple garments that I wear."

"And your garments," inquired the master, "what would you do if they were to come between you and your peace?"

Without even a moment's doubt, the woman rose before the master, loosened the waist belt around her, and allowed the garments to fall to the ground. Immediately, the master made a hand gesture. Two disciples came forward and wrapped her in a single garment of pure silk. The master rose to his feet. Standing in front of the woman, he placed his arms around her neck and fastened a fine silver chain there. Connected to the chain was a single, unadorned silver star that rested on her bosom.

The star glistened brilliantly. A ray of sunlight broke through the shade of the tree, touching the woman's face. To the many, she seemed transformed before their eyes.

The master spoke to her in a tone that only the nearest standing by could hear.

Venus I name you, Venus you are

Before us you rise, like a

bright morning star

This is your moment out of time for release

To rise above the many and find your peace

He kissed her on the brow.

Turning to the multitude, the master proclaimed with an authority that seemed to shake the very foundations of the earth. "Never have I seen faith as great as this among the kindred. For on this day, one among you has vowed to forgo all attachments this world presents as peace offerings. And this one among you has laid down all pride that the ego argues for in the name of self-preservation, so that The Way to peace might be recognized. I tell you the truth, on this very day, one among you has entered the road that leads to peace eternal. What can be taken from this one that she could claim as a painful loss if she claims nothing for herself but her inheritance?"

To this question, no one said a word. But all remained in reverent awe before the star.

Salvation's Way

"Master!" exclaimed a surprised seeker, who was following the master along The Way. "How can you say that 'expectations' get in the way of a peaceful mind? You have to have expectations to make sure things happen!"

The master stopped, turned to look into her eyes and stated gently, "Little one, don't worry. If you walk with me, you won't walk through your fear alone."

"Master?" asked a disciple who was listening in. "You said that each of us has to work out our own salvation. How can you do for her what she won't do for herself?"

The master stated simply, "Her walk is a demonstration of her work. The extension of love to a call for help does the rest. And," added the master, "to see the call in another is your walk in seeing your own salvation at work."

Interrupted
By The Way

One day a worried skeptic approached the master to make a point.

"Sir," the skeptic apprehensively stammered, "all these things you talk about sound so nice and true, but I've got so many problems that I can't . . ."

"Do you own a house?" interrupted the master.

"Yes, but . . ."

"Do you have a job?" continued the master, as if to interrogate him.

"Yes, but . . ."

"Do you have a car?" continued the master.

The skeptic angrily bit his tongue for a moment. The master waited calmly for the skeptic to make his standard response of "Yes, but..." (as the master knew he eventually would), and interrupted the inevitable words a fourth time.[34]

"And do you socialize with many prominent acquaintances?"

Giving up any attempt to argue, the skeptic finally

---

[34]Chronic worrying is an obsessive cycle. Interrupting it with a thought of truth is the immediate solution.

resigned with a "yes." He also decided to step back and do something different. He decided to listen.

Sensing the skeptic's resignation, the master shifted into a quiet and gentle tone of voice. "And, with all this, you still worry. In spite of your attempts to control, everything has always worked itself out. But instead of being grateful, you choose to worry. Tell me," asked the master genuinely, "What is one thing you do always?"

Perplexed by the question, the skeptic stammered, "Well . . . uh . . . I, uh . . . I'm not really sure."

"You breathe, don't you?" asked the master playfully, "Almost as much as you obsess." He laughed. "Now when you find yourself with a problem, a worry, mind you, think of your breathing."

"But that's hard to do when I'm thinking about all my problems," responded the skeptic.

"No, it's not," stated the master. "Thinking about a problem is not really thinking at all."

"How can you say that?" responded the provoked skeptic.

"Easily," continued the master boldly, as if to tease. "When you worry about what might happen, it's about something that isn't. Thinking about something that isn't is not thinking, it's mis-thought."

"But I can think of times when my worries happen," spoke the skeptic, justifying his thought process.

With humor evident in his voice, the master

responded, "Even a broken clock is correct twice a day. However, what happens, happens. But how you decide to interpret what happens will be your experience. If you worry about what might be, you will hold it up before your eyes until you can say with prophetic authority, 'See, look there, that proves I have a problem!' What you do not realize is that you are choosing to find what your mind is anticipating it will see.[35] In this case—your particular worry. And poof, like magic, it's there! However, your problem is not magical. It is your thinking reflected back by any available circumstance. That's not thinking, that's single minded mis-thought looking back at you."

"So whenever you find yourself in a state of mis-thought," summarized the master, "focus on your breathing, it will clarify things for you."[36]

That day, the skeptic became a seeker of The Way.

---

[35]The power of the mind to selectively perceive.

[36]Interrupting this cycle allows the worrier room for a different thought.

Accepting The Way

One day a teacher was addressing the master about a personally disappointing situation. Working on an attitude of acceptance, the teacher stated with a sigh, "Oh, well, I suppose it was meant to be."

"Indulge an old man," remarked the master. "Just for the sake of conversation, what's the opposite of 'meant to be'?"

"Well, I suppose it would be 'wasn't meant to be,'" answered the teacher, wondering what the master was up to.

"What's the step beyond all duality of thought?"

Thoughtfully, the teacher replied, "Well, I don't know. What is it?"

The master stated emphatically, "Whether it's meant to be or not is irrelevant to 'what is'! Yes, it is true," continued the master, "that every thing has a reason until..."[37]

The master paused for a short moment, as if to leave the teacher hanging, "...*until* you recognize that no reason is necessary. As was said of old," continued the master, "if you understand, things are the way they are. If you do not understand, things are the way they are."[38]

---

[37]The understanding of what the reason is makes what happens irrelevant because the reason is the lesson.

[38]An old Zen proverb.

The Ego's Way

One day while the master was walking along The Way, he came to a place where a community disaster had occurred.

Death, pain and fear permeated the scene. Many worked feverishly to unearth victims, both living and dead. The master, along with the disciples, worked late into the night to help comfort the hurt and traumatized.

By morning, a professional rescue operation was in place, and the master could take a break.

A disciple asked, "Master, how can a loving God—as you describe Him—allow such bad things to happen?"

"What bad things did God allow to happen?" asked the

master, recognizing a timeless teaching opportunity.

"Well, just like this disaster," continued the disciple, "all kinds of tragedies are constantly happening in the world, like floods, hurricanes, tornadoes, earthquakes, mudslides, fires, war, diseases of all kinds. Master, the list is endless."

"You are right to say that the list is endless," responded the master, "but to say that God allows, or even causes such things is a belief only supported by madness, endless madness." The master chuckled at his unintended play on words.

"But, master, the world was created by God!" the disciple stated in confusion.

"Was it?" All were silent, waiting for the master to continue. "All that you perceive is temporary, is it not?" questioned the master. "Look around you, show me something that has eternal value." The disciples could show the master nothing.

"Because it was written somewhere that God created all that you perceive does not make it true as much as it makes someone's perception into ink on paper. But this is a hard concept for the ego to accept, because it needs a kingdom of its own to survive. And to have this kingdom, it needs to fool you into believing that its place of residency, the world you experience through the five senses, has something to do with God. In this way does the ego give itself legitimacy. You need the ego, so it seems, to survive because the world God created, as the ego prescribes, is constantly fraught with worry, anger and fear, life-and-death decisions. That is also why many have a fearful concept of a God who allows tragedy and judges with punishment."

"And still," continued the master, "you look for the Kingdom of God in a place it will never be found—why? Because you are the Kingdom God created. It is not out there to be found, and the ego does not want you to know this. Because the spirit that you are is the Kingdom God created, God does not participate in the dream that suggests that the Kingdom of God is something or somewhere else. He does not recognize anything that is temporal or not real. It is not real because what God creates is eternal. What you are is beyond the trappings of the temporal. But you have seduced yourself into accepting the temporal flash in a pan as your identity, as you. The ego needs you to believe this is all true or else it is out of a job. We make the dream seem meaningfully real by putting our own concept of God into it—giving God such roles as those of judge, jury, jailer and executioner. Now it is God that is meting out gifts and punishments as He sees fit, and us explaining God's contradictions as 'mysterious ways' by saying 'it was meant to be.' You say 'this is a loving God' in wonder and confusion, sacrificing common sense at the altar of the ego. Only a madman lost in a nightmare could believe this."

"What is it we are to believe, master?"

"That your Father could never abandon what he created perfect out of love. The very definition and nature of love is that which could never abandon itself. If it could abandon itself, it would not be love that you are experiencing, but rather something of the ego's making. It is true that you, the prodigal son,[39] went off to a foreign land and squandered your inheritance in loose living. Yet, when you come back to your senses, when you wake up, you will find that you never left the arms of your Father. Here I will speak plainly. The story was never to be about the prodigal son. It is the story of the Ever-loving Father."

"And if it be true," continued the master, "that you cannot oppose the Will of God except in a dream of vain imaginings, then when you finally awaken from your dream of nothingness, the dream God does not know, the dream you made for your little ego-kingdom to be separate from God, the dream you took as fearfully real, you will awaken to love."

Some among the crowd became restless and spoke among themselves. Others began to leave. They did not want to hear about God in this way. This was not the way they were taught about God. It went against everything they believed about their experience of the world and how the world was made. But most of all and unknown to them, they feared love.

"And here again, I will speak to you plainly. There is no Hell except that which you make out of your dream of nothingness. That hell can be a concept born out of a perfect creation of love is merely the ego's madness attempting to secure a kingdom in the ever-changing nothingness. No wonder the Creator of Love is feared. It

---

[39]Luke chapter 15, vs. 11-32

is believed that He has allowed for a place of punishment, suffering, loss and death. Oh, yes, let's add a place for beautiful sunsets, pristine waterfalls and starry nights of romance so the ego can hide behind God's beautiful creation of contradiction. Nevertheless, our dreams are places to experience the fear of love until we decide to see our dream as meaningless chaos because it is separate from God's perfection."

"And so," ended the master, "for those who need to be saved from Hell, so be it. Yet, be ye aware it is the making of your hell and yours alone that you need to be saved from."

The master rose from his break, seeking once again to help any in need.

The Way
Through
Flowers

"Master," stated the young aspirant, "you speak much of all of this being just a dream. If that is so, then what is to be taken seriously?"

"Of value is only that which reminds you of your awakening beyond the dream. Beyond that, nothing matters."

"But, master, what about a legacy of generosity, compassion and good deeds?"

"As ends, for their own sake, they are meaningless. As a means for working out your own salvation, they can be helpful. However, be not deceived with ego nobility. It is not about making the dream better; it is about waking from your dream. This is your individual responsibility—to see the ego's deception for what it is . . . a dream of nothingness. And because you have deceived yourself into believing nothing is something, you must work with this so-called 'something' until it teaches you that it was nothing. You don't need a sword to cut a path through a meadow of flowers."[40]

---

[40]A paraphrase of John Lennon's lyrics from "Whatever Gets You Through the Night."

Nothing's Way

Doing something about nothing
Makes nothing seem like something.

When nothing seems like something
You have to do something about it.

Until you see it as it is.
Nothing.

The Paradox Of The Way

One cool fall evening while sitting around a fire, two teachers were arguing over the academics of what a "renunciate" was. One argued that a renunciate was one who owns nothing and carries nothing along the journey. The other defended her position that a renunciate can have things, but must cultivate an attitude of detachment from them. Finally, out of frustration at not being able to resolve their differences,[41] they decided together (which was an amazing accomplishment for these two) to ask the master to set things straight.

Approaching the master, who was quietly resting just outside of the firelight, they respectfully asked, "Master, tell us, who is right on this matter?"

Without stirring from his rest, the master replied with

---

[41]Trying to change another's mind is the ingredient necessary for any argument.

stoic disinterest, "A renunciate is one who has nothing to renounce. By laying down the position of renunciation, you are free to enjoy times of plenty as well as times of lack."[42]

Not satisfied with an answer that did not win the argument for either side, the teachers pressed the master again, asking, "Tell us, who is right here?"

The master sat up against a boulder, wrapping himself in a blanket to keep warm. He looked thoughtfully at each before speaking, "For you two, a renunciate is one who defends no position. For what you protect, you are attached to and value as your own, and therefore must defend from loss. If you truly own it not, why do you fight to defend it? Now, tell me," instructed the master, "which one of you will claim to be right?"

The teachers quietly went back to their own business around the fire.

---

[42]The true renunciate looks at the heart of each matter rather than judging according to appearances. In this way a true renunciate gives up the judgment of "forms" rather than just giving up the forms themselves. There are endless variations of "forms." This does not imply endless variations on content. There is only one content. This is the final lesson.

Symbols Along The Way

One day the
master performed
a ceremony[43]
using various
rituals, herbs and
elements of the
earth.

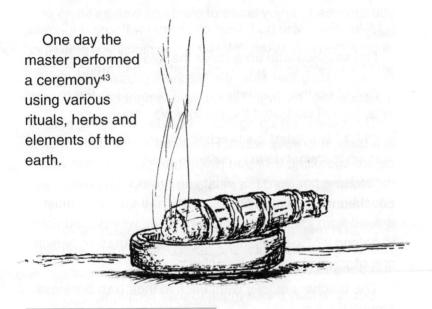

---

[43]The natural experience of any initiation is recognized by an
expansive awareness of personal peace. Growing awareness is a
process that realizes that peace of mind has *nothing* to do with
external circumstances. This helps you manifest a desire to let go of
any need to "try" to control the world of people, things and events.
Your sense of release is preceded by a disorientation of frustration. If
you look honestly at your frustration, you will hear it say to you; "None
of my old ways, values, and thoughts are working anymore." No more
do they elicit personal satisfaction. Yet, to go forward into the
unknown seems to encompass fearful possibilities. The unknown is
not in the hands of the old familiar way. Such is the initiate's dilemma
and prerequisite when the choice is clearly seen. Purification is a
process of resolving to forgo control of your personal destiny. This
resolve opens doors you never knew were there. Now your purpose
to yourself and your community can unfold. Ceremonial initiations and
community witness can be helpful to support your journey of
purification. Initiations reflect and honor your experience of
participation in the larger picture.

The occasion honored a disciple's growth in one-mindedness.

A teacher, who had been observing with great interest, approached and asked, "Master, those rituals you performed and those symbols you used, what do they mean?"

"What do they mean to whom?" responded the master, knowing full well what the teacher was asking.

"Well," hesitated the teacher, unsure what the master was up to, "what do they mean to you?"

"Nothing," replied the master, enjoying the teacher's bewilderment.

"Huh?" responded the teacher in confusion. After collecting her thoughts, she asked, "Well, then, why did you perform them?"

Because they mean much to their recipient."

"But not to you?" asked the teacher with continued puzzlement.

The master smiled and began this story:

"Once there was a woman who was well-known in her community for the use of symbols of power for ceremonial healing. She also had a gift for facilitating healing.

A man, desiring this gift for personal gain, broke into her house. Not understanding that this gift had nothing to do with the manipulation of earth symbols, he took the sacred symbols that the woman used in her ceremonies.

His fellow robber admonished him, saying, 'Don't take those! You will steal her heart's desire, which will haunt you until you are found.'[44] But he did not heed the warning of his fellow robber and took the sacred symbols for himself.

When the woman came home and realized what had happened, a great weight was lifted from her heart. She had struggled for release from the power of her sacred symbols, but was afraid to give them up because she so strongly identified with them. Through her prayers, help had come. Her burden had been lifted. Rejoicing that this loss was actually her gain,[45] she called her friends to join her in celebration. What was once used for her healing was no longer necessary. She had grown beyond their original intent."

"And so, I say," concluded the master, "those who live in the world relate to the things of the world by giving meaning to those things according to their need. Therefore, let nothing possess you through the meaning you fix upon it!"

"What about you?" asked the teacher, wondering how the master fit into this explanation.

"Those who are not in the world relate not to that which has no meaning in itself. In this way do all things become a matter of convenience. In that understanding, all things can serve a purpose in healing."

---

[44]Those who use an earth symbol as a means to personal power will be enslaved by the magic they gave that symbol until they resolve to release themselves from the symbol to which they gave their power.
[45]Lack of value was being recognized.

Temptations
Along The Way

One rainy day, a seeker approached the master to ask a question. Hoping to justify a personal position, the seeker disguised her agenda behind nice words. "Kind sir," the seeker started, "many among the wise say that if one prospers within oneself, then one will prosper financially. What do you say?"

Seeing through the seeker's words to her self-serving agenda, the master replied, "If you prosper within yourself, you have no need to think of prospering financially."

Not satisfied with the master's words, the seeker exposed her position by asserting, "But master, can't money be useful as a help to one's happiness?"

The master responded briskly, "Be careful with money and its subtleties. Deceive yourself no more. Your search for money as a means to happiness will bring you disappointment. Those who are truly happy are so

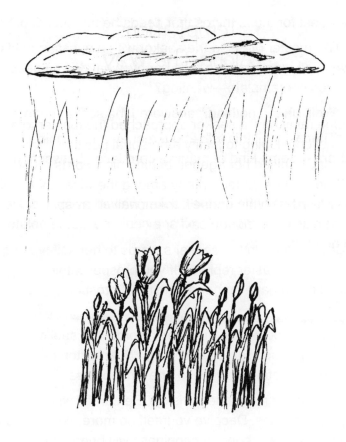

because they have prospered from within. There is no disappointment in this because it does not depend on the whims of anything outside of themselves. Nor do they risk any loss from being robbed. For what can be taken from you if you value it not? I am not saying your choices will always be easy, but The Way is simple to understand. In itself, green slips of numbered paper and shiny metal disks and all their subtleties are not evil. It is the quest for these things that needs be transcended."

The master pressed the seeker with a question of his own. "Tell me, if you are truly happy, what do you need—or even contemplate—wanting?"

"Well, uh . . . nothing," answered the seeker honestly.

"Then why all this talk about money and happiness as if there is some kind of magical correlation between the two?"

With a heavy heart, the seeker walked away. Her life was invested in money, and she could not contemplate an alternative way.

The Way Through Deception

"Master, tell us about those who deceive others. Are they not among the least beloved in the Kingdom of God?"

"Always remember that if you see deception in another, it is because you have deceived yourself first."

"What do you mean 'we have deceived ourselves first'?" protested one of the disciples.

"To not see those who deceive others as being in a place of self-deception is self-deception on your part. It is self-deception because it is judgment of another that breeds conflict rather than peace within you. Remember this and you allow a way to forgive the self-deception you did not see in yourself."

Minding Your Way

One day the master was teaching on the attitude of the carefree life.

A doubter rose up from among the crowd, pointing his finger and directing many words of anger at the master. The master remained quiet and relaxed. Upon finishing his tirade, the doubter stomped away. The master picked up his teaching on the attitude of the carefree life where he had left off—as if nothing had happened. After the crowd dispersed, the disciples came together and talked about the day's events.

Finally, one of the disciples asked, "Master, why did you not respond to the doubter's disrespectful tone of voice towards you?"

"Tell me," asked the master, "what did that one's comments say about him?"

"That he is very unhappy," responded a perceptive disciple.

"Well said!" replied the master. "Knowing that much about that one, tell me, what do his comments of anger towards me have to do with me?"

The disciples pondered this question amongst themselves. Finally they came up with a simple answer: "Really nothing."

"Do not involve yourself with affairs that do not belong to you; it will preserve your peace."[46]

---

[46]What people think of you is none of your business.

The Essence Of The Way

One day the master was giving a discourse on the essence of Self . . . beyond all the trappings, lures, temptations, and adornments of false association. Some from among the gathering crowd confused themselves by what they thought they heard the master say.

"How can you say I am not a body!" stated one, feeling threatened by his own ideas of what he thought he had heard the master say. "Look at the obvious. Don't I have hands for touching and legs for walking? Don't I have eyes for seeing and ears for hearing? Isn't it obvious to you that I have a mouth for speaking?" So intense were the words of this one that beads of sweat formed on his brow. He had a strong need to convince himself.

"I will ask you a simple question that all must ask in their own way and time," spoke the master. "It is a question of choice between life and death." The large crowd became quietly captive. "Now tell me," continued the master, "when the body breathes no more, do you cease to be?"

The doubter was confounded by the question.

A seeker standing by understood the nature of the question. She cautiously and curiously addressed the master. "What if one was to say we die when our bodies die?"

"Then your time is short-lived, accounting for nothing, and this conversation is meaningless," said the master with a smile.

"What if I wanted to say, 'I do not stay with the body I have'?" continued the curious seeker, thoughtfully.

"Then you begin to understand that there is something about you that is more than what you appear to be, making your time here dependent upon the understanding of your final lesson," the master stated.

"What would that final lesson be?" the curious seeker asked.

"You will know what it is when you are ready to have it," responded the master.

"To better understand, we must go back to our beginnings," expounded the master, "In the beginning, time was not so, nor was humankind. As was written of old, humankind began thusly: 'Then God said, Let us make humankind in Our image according to Our likeness.[47] And in God's image are God's children created.' Now either God is a God of flesh and bone, created in *our* image, or God's children are spirit, an

---

[47] A loose translation of Genesis 1:26 (NAS) Because "Being Itself" is One, it is beyond any idea of a duality of individual consciousness. There is no reality apart from or in opposition to "God is."

extension of God, merely forgetful of their true identities. The answer is further clarified in what was also said of old and still stands to this day: 'God is Spirit, and those who worship Him must worship in Spirit and in Truth.'"[48]

The seeker nodded in understanding as the master continued to expound. "Spirit is the unifying force continually reminding us of our direct connection with God." Around them, some in the gathered throng nodded as they began to recall their own connections with God.

"However, guilt, conscious and unconscious, is the result of your belief that you can oppose the will of God and succeed. Because of this strange belief, you have become obsessed with hiding your guilt. Trying to get rid of it, you have projected it into the idea of "body as self." Having forgotten our relationship with our Source, we make a god in our own image, a god that punishes guilt, and we begin to believe that it is the body—the place of guilt's domain—that must be punished. This is how the mind uses the body as a witness to the lie that we have severed our connection with God."

"How can this be possible?" the master asked rhetorically, not expecting an answer from the mesmerized crowd. "The Great Separation is the detour into fear, making our world an illusion of nothingness, the nightmare from which all struggle to awaken. You are still with God and do not know it."

The master continued his discourse saying, "Your

---

[48]John 4:23-25 (NAS)

body is merely a *vehicle* through the forgetfulness of space and time. It is nothing more and nothing less. However, the power of your mind is such that what you decide, you will experience. Focus on the body as 'you,' and you choose to limit life to what is dictated by your body. Your life will be separate, needy and ever-changing, unknown to the Self we all share because you decided to limit your understanding to only what is experienced in this vehicle of change. Your experience of life becomes a path from being born in pain to fearing death in pain." The master wondered if any in the crowd understood his words. Knowing not to despair, he continued.

"However, because your body is merely a witness to the change of dust to dust, healing is of the mind. Unless you use your vehicle—your body—as a reminder that all true healing is in the changing of your mind, your inevitable destination will be to fear change as personally meaningful."

The Way Of Healing

A woman, confined to a wheelchair for many long years, besought the master for a healing. Looking into her eyes, the master could see that she was guilt-ridden as to how she had lived her life.

The master asked, "God, who does not see your life as you see it, but only sees His creation of love that you are, holds what sin against you?"

Taken aback by what the master said, the lady responded, "When you say it that way, what sin could there be that God could hold against me?"

"I asked you first," the master shot back playfully.

"Well," the lady stated thoughtfully, "He holds no sin against me."

"Though you may never walk again," stated the master, "you have the power of your mind to change your mind, to forgive yourself for the sins you never committed except in the imaginings of your sleepy dream. And as you forgive what never occurred, you work out your salvation towards waking up to the arms of God that you never left. Without guilt, you are free to love all of God's creation because you remember the essence of what you are through God's eyes, rather than your eyes. This is the miracle of rising above the dust of the body, when healing comes to your mind."

"When healing comes to my mind?" questioned the woman.

"You are not the car you drive," continued the master. "Many forget this until the car breaks down and they have to get it fixed. No matter how many times you fix it, one day it ends up in the junkyard. And now I say this to put all arguments to rest. You are not the lump of metal that ends up in the junkyard. You are the Spirit of God that seemed to inhabit it for a short time. Whether you are in a wheelchair or not is not the relevant factor. But when you allow your body its proper function, no matter what its condition seems to be, it will be of help to you in your unified purpose for mind's healing. If you still do not fully understand your body's proper role, do not rush like a fool to decide what it is. Instead, let your body's purpose be shown to you, so it can be used as a means of healing rather than a witness to fear, pain, and death. I do not deny that in the illusion, healings of the body seem to occur. But if your goal is to heal the body, in the end, it will fail you and die. Do not fear. For you are more than the body you appear to inhabit. To shed this body is like taking off your old clothing to be laid aside for the new. 'Birth' becomes the putting on of the new after the shedding of the old."

At this point, the first among the crowd to insist upon his limitations as a body rose up. "What do you mean birth comes after death! Everyone knows that people are born first, and then they die. That's the way it is!" Some in the crowd, who had stood up to leave in anger at the master's last words, paused to hear the master's reply.

"Here's the truth. Even in the changing of your 'clothing', like the shedding of a snake's skin, the essence of You is never broken. Your separation from God has not occurred. Your separation is but the imaginings of a sleepy dreamer lost in a nightmare of thoughts, separate from the memory of the original thought God shares with you. Although God shares His thoughts with you continuously, the part of your mind that thinks separately from God is not aware of this, because it thinks it thinks.[49] Like this wheelchair-bound woman, when you forgive the part of your mind that is unknowingly lost in the dream of its own thinking and the experience of its thought that follows, you will wake up from your dream realizing nothing has really occurred. This is the final lesson."

Discussion broke out among the crowd. The master calmly proceeded, never lifting his voice. "The amount of time you spend here is the amount of time it takes you to learn your final lesson: that death is but your release from the idea of yourself as a body. Your birth is but your awakening to the essence you are in God. There is no birth or death."

---

[49]What is any thought separate from God? It is but an experience of nothingness lost in the thought of its own delusion.

"And so I say to you all," summarized the master, "the power of your mind decides what you will experience. Look upon yourself as a body, and you become invested in the experience of death. Look beyond the dust of time, and you invite the experiences that prepare you for your awakening from your forgetfulness of what you thought you were."

Upon the end of this discourse, the master moved away, seeking seclusion from the crowd.

Enlightenment's Way

"Enlightenment is to awaken from the dream."

"Which means?"

"You don't take the dream seriously any more . . . and then you remember joy.[50] In the meantime, perceive yourself as waking up."

---

[50]Joy is objective, because it is not subject to the interpretation of any outside influences (stimuli) that gives us all the other feelings. Joy is the expression of your true nature—waiting for you to remember that you are free to let go of all the subjective thoughts of evaluation, interpretation and judgment that seem to give the experience of meaning.

The Way Of The Spirit

"Master, how does the Spirit of God work in the world?"

"The Spirit of God does not work in the world." To the amusement of the master, his comment befuddled the disciples.

"But people are always praying for the Spirit of God to work in the world," protested one disciple.

"What world?" asked the master, continuing to play.

The disciples looked at him in confusion. "Please explain?" they asked.

"Remember," started the master, "the world is not real, but rather a mirage, *an effect* of the mind that made it in a dream. Therefore, don't look for the Spirit of God in the effects of a mis-thought that you have mistakenly taken as real. Rather look for the Spirit of God in the mind that made the mis-thought. Your correction will never come to you through the world of effects—except as a reflection that tells the mind that it made the effects. That is how the Spirit of God can use what you have taken as a means to deceive yourself for an opportunity to remember true cause.

Seeing the bewilderment on the faces of many who gathered 'round, the master rephrased his comments. "In other words," stated the master, "the world of effects will never correct your mis-thought; it will only *reflect* the effects of the mis-thought that the mind made. Believing the effects of mind's error to be cause (the world), the mind will be caught in a cycle of self-deception, unable to see its way out and thus lost. But the Spirit of God can use the effects of your deceptive mis-thoughts as an opportunity to remind you that *your mind* is the true cause of the world. But it is up to you, when you are sick and tired of being sick and tired, to turn your thoughts over to the direction of the Spirit of Truth so He can correct not the dream, but the mind that made the dream. *It is not up to you to choose what your lessons should be.* But it is up to you *when* you will choose to learn the lesson presented to you in your everyday life."

The Way Of
Salvation

During a lively conversation about the simplicity of salvation, the master concluded, "Because God does not see you as lost, no one but you can save you for you."

"That's not true!" protested a deeply religious believer. "It is only God who can save us!"

"Well, then," added the master, "you're saved."

"Well . . . " hesitated the religious believer, "it's not that simple."

"Oh?" questioned the master. "Then you're not saved?"

"Well, no. I mean, yes," expressed the confused religious believer. "I am saved but . . . "

"If you are saved," interrupted the master, "how come you still feel anger, confusion and fear?"

"Because I don't always believe that I am saved," the religious believer answered thoughtfully.

"Like I said," stated the master, "because God does not see you as lost, no one but you can save you for you."

Entrapment's Way

There was one who approached the master with the intent of ensnaring him. "Master," he said with feigned sincerity, "it is said that you know all things. However, it was also said of old, 'Those who know do not talk about it. Those who talk about it do not know.'[51] So tell me, why do you talk about it?"

The master shrugged. "Because you asked?"

---

[51]The Tao De Ching

Repeating The Way

A seeker asked, "Master, often you say the same things, just in different ways. Why is that?"

The master smiled with an inner delight and responded, "When *the only function meaningful in time is forgiveness*, there isn't much else to talk about."

This time the seeker pressed, "But why the repetition?"

"Every one of you has more than one example of a time when you mistook someone the wrong way, reacted to your interpretation of them as if it were true, had a problem with them because you did not recognize you were merely reacting to your own misinterpretation, eventually realized your mistake, and all of a sudden like a miracle . . ." the master gestured dramatically, "...the 'big' problem was gone. And still you are slow to generalize this lesson to every area of your life. Therefore, repeating the lesson seems to be the necessity...until you get it."

Challenged
By The Way

The question is not "Is there life after death?"

The question is "Is there death?"

Time's Way

One day, away from the pursuing crowd, the master rested under a large oak tree. It was the autumn of the tree's life, and the leaves were going through their colorful changes.

The disciples were just a short distance off, having a lively conversation. Finally, they approached the master for a comment.

"Master," they interrupted, "tell us of reincarnation—is it true?"

Turning his back to the disciples, the master responded briefly. "In truth, reincarnation is unnecessary. In time, it appears as a painful obligation."

This did not abate the confusion among the disciples. Risking the displeasure the master might take toward the interruption, one of the disciples was chosen to ask as delicately as possible, "Could you explain? We don't understand."

The master sat up, yawned and stretched. Gesturing to Old Mr. Oak, he began, "In the spring, this tree buds and blossoms, bearing fruit of its kind in the summer.

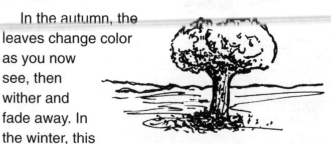

In the autumn, the leaves change color as you now see, then wither and fade away. In the winter, this tree appears dormant... and would like some quiet shut-eye," concluded the master, once again lying down and turning onto his side, away from the disciples.

It became apparent to the disciples that the master had explained his piece. But still, they remained in a fog. Unabashed, they persisted. "Could you make it clearer for us what you mean?"

The master sat up, mumbling irritably. Seeing them seated around him softened his displeasure. These were the ones with whom he laughed and cried, and whom he loved as his own. Though he was exhausted, how could he resist their persistence in wanting to know?

"Now listen carefully," he started, "for I say this without riddle: This tree is your body. The springtime of this tree signifies new life, the budding of your physical birth. Blossoming into the fruits of its kind is the growth and maturity of your summer. The autumn of your life demonstrates the colorful expressions of wisdom through experience, until winter claims you back. Now tell me," asked the master, looking about at the disciples, "through this cycle, did this tree die?"

"No!" resounded the disciples.

"How do you know?" asked the master.

"Because it will bud again in the spring," they replied.

"Yes! And so I tell you a truth; even though this tree goes through its changes, doing its dance year after year, the spirit of this tree remains unchanged. You are not the part of the tree that changes year after year. You are the spirit of the tree that remains unchanged. When the spirit of the tree finally realizes from its yearly cycles that it was always in its center, it will say to itself, 'I finally choose to lay this body down once and for all time. No more do I make myself a victim of time's way.'"

"Time makes reincarnation seem like a painful obligation, until you realize that you have never left your center. You only imagined so."

Without hesitation, the master went back to resting with Old Mr. Oak.

Freedom's Way

"What do you believe in?" asked the cynic.

"I don't believe in anything."

Attempting to trap the master in a paradox, the cynic stated, "To not believe in anything is a belief."

The master asked mischievously, "What is there in the absence of belief?"

"Well, I don't know."

"That is why one has to believe," directed the master. "Those who know they need not know, know they need not believe."[52]

---

[52]You need faith to believe in what you do not know.

Way Beyond Belief

"Your philosophy on life is very interesting."

"It's not a philosophy."

"Why not?"

"I don't believe it."

Fooled Along The Way

"What do you believe about evil?"[53] asked a seeker.

"I don't know evil."

"Would you explain?"

"God is everything that is changeless. What's the opposite of everything?"

"Nothing."

"I don't know nothing."

"But surely you see evil in the world!" challenged a skeptic.

"What world? Those who believe in evil are makers and partakers of the world. Those who know no evil know not the world and are therefore counted as innocent. It has been said before, 'Beware of Maya.'[54] But now I say to you: Be not on guard against nothing. Rather, beware of your ability to make nothing seem like something."

---

[53]Is evil real? This is a question limited to the experience of selective perception. All meanings start with the mind that first thought them. You will select and find what you first believed to be true. That is why evil is not objective, but rather a subjective choice to see circumstances that way. You will experience evil if that is what you asked to find. "Seek and you shall find" is not just a promise. It's a choice. If hell is the home you ask for, karma will be your means.

[54]Maya is the power of illusion; the experience of ever-shifting forms (that is, the whole world of material, temporal existence), perceived through the senses as separate selves and things, not realizing that all separate existences are essentially unreal - Hinduism.

Grief's Way

"Master!" exclaimed a frustrated disciple. "I get the idea of not grieving the inevitable, and that we grieve it because we cultivate a relationship of attachment, even ownership, to that which is not ours to own. I can see that we grieve because we lie to ourselves about the truth of the matter! And because death is inevitable, we are to embrace[55] it with celebration and joy. But here's my problem: as I have gotten older, my friends and colleagues have people dying all around them. So all around me, all I hear are tearful stories of people dying and all the drama and grief that go along with that. Sometimes it drives me crazy. I just want to scream at them to tell them 'It's not real!' But I know not to fight with someone who is grieving his or her illusion! But why do they refuse to get it?" The disciple raised his voice to exclaim, "Everybody dies!"

The master looked into this one's eyes and smiled in remembrance. "Dear one, why are you so concerned about how others grieve their illusions . . . unless those illusions are also yours?" queried the master.

"Your frustration is just another form of masked anger, and anger is *always* a response to a perceived threat of

---

[55]To embrace is the last step prior to seeing its irrelevance in the light of God's plan. And God's plan? Well actually, God needs no plan in the light of the fact that you are God's child, eternally innocent and changeless.

180

loss. And loss *always* involves the death of an illusion. If death is not real, this has to be true. In your case, you have an 'attachment' to a *belief* that people should think the way you do about death. And you know your belief is an illusion because it does what all illusions do. It lulls you from your peace of mind into misery. You are merely grieving how you think another should think. You are just like the one you think you are different from. 'Embrace it,' you say. I say, why do you not rejoice in the birth of every sunrise and grieve the death of every sunset?"

"Master," expressed the disciple thoughtfully, "everybody knows these things are everyday occurrences."

"So is death. If you allow the exception by making one illusion be more real than another, it all becomes real to you," the master pointed out. "And what do those who grieve teach you?"

The disciple thought for a brief second . . . "They teach me that I have allowed their illusion to become a belief that is real to me."

"And?" chided the master playfully.

"And that I grieve its death?" questioned the disciple, looking into the master's eyes.

"And?" chided the master again.

"They teach me tolerance," spoke the disciple with reluctance.

"And?" prodded the master playfully.

"I guess," hesitated the disciple, "I guess they teach me patience."

"Which makes them your . . ." prompted the master.

"...teachers," the disciple swallowed.

"You can thank them by being present and quiet in their moment of grief. And if they invite you to be otherwise, you can embrace them with celebration and joy."

Death's Way

"Master, your mother died. Why do you not mourn?"

"Because I, along with her, have died."

"I don't understand,"

"Do you yet not know that the self[56] that dies in the arms of non-existence allows for your birth to the Greater Self? Therefore, through the death of self, one sees the life of all. My mother is not dead. But until you die to your make-believe self,[57] all will die to you."

---

[56]Ego

[57]Death always involves the burial of an illusion. Death is an illusion. Therefore, the death of your make-believe self (ego) is your release to 'The You' we all share.

Opportunity's Way

"If only I would have done it differently," stated the self-disappointing student, "I wouldn't be here now . . . in this mess."

"This is where you're supposed to be," challenged the master.

"How can you say that? How do you know?" inquired the student in a stressed tone of voice.

"How long will I remain here to teach what a child already knows?" wondered the master. "Self-acceptance rests in the fact that this is where you're supposed to be, dealing with how you see what you see, until you see it differently."

"Yes, but I don't seem to be learning from my mistakes," countered the frustrated student, arguing with himself.

"Trying to reach perfection in terms of behavior is not only ridiculous but is also impossible. Your willingness to receive correction is the only thing that is necessary. Besides," chided the master playfully, "this is where you are. If you weren't supposed to be here, you would be somewhere else, thinking, 'If *only* I would have done it differently, I wouldn't be here now.' But here you are, here now to learn a lesson, should you so choose. Think about being somewhere else, and you miss the gift before you here and now."

The Way Of Expectations

While the master was speaking on the many blessings that are found along The Way, one from among the crowd, tempted by the expectations of life's way, interrupted with a protest.

"Master, I have prayed much for these blessings you talk about, but have yet to see any of them materialize! How can you say that God is an ever-present blessing when I feel He has abandoned me?"

The master turned to look at the man. He could see that the man was agitated and hungry for an argument. The master proceeded by calmly leaning towards the man and speaking softly.

"There once was a man who whispered 'God, speak to me,' and a meadowlark sang.

But the man did not hear."

The master continued by stepping back and raising his voice.

"So the man yelled, 'God, speak to me,' and the thunder rolled across the sky.

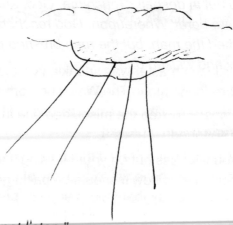

But the man did not listen."

The master comically looked around the people standing by as if looking for something misplaced.

"Then the man looked around and said, 'God, let me see You,' and a star shone brightly.

But the man did not notice."

The master continued, even more loudly:

"And the man shouted, 'God show me a miracle!' and a life was born. But the man did not know. So the man

---

[58]Drawing by Magdalena B. Kuntscher.

cried out in despair, 'Touch me, God, and let me know you are here!' Whereupon, God reached down and touched the man, but the man brushed the butterfly away and walked on." [59]

The master looked the misguided one in the face, and his eyes softened.

"You will miss out on your blessing if you have expectations of how it should be packaged."

---

[59]Anonymous

Sharing The Way

"What do you seek?" asked the master of one who was intent on having an audience with him.

"Master, I seek the gift of enlightenment!" returned the ecstatic reply.[60]

"Seek it not as a gift!" exclaimed the master for all around to hear. "Rather, seek the Source of All Gifts, so that in return you may have all gifts to share."

---

[60]Seekers of experience fall into this category. Caution is needed here because the unaware do not realize to what extent they decide their own experiences through desire. The decision to participate in the One is a decision to not decide what your experience should be. Be open, be responsive, don't decide…and what you need, you will find as gifts to give along your way.

Masters Of The Way

Because he lives beyond the answer,
The master is free to redirect the student to seek truth.

Because he lives beyond thought,
The master is free to respond to the student according to
the need of any moment.

Because he lives beyond the idea of ego,
The master is free to accompany the student through any
conversation, beyond the need to defend.

Because he lives beyond the desire to possess,
The master is free to facilitate healing with whatever is
provided for him.

Because he lives today within the oneness of peace,
The master knows neither the consequence of tomorrow
nor guilt of yesterday.

Therefore, the master is free to extend healing through
all that is seen, thought and done.

The Door Way

"I will not always be with you as you see me now."

"Master, where are we to go, what are we to do when you go?"[61]

"When the door opens before you, walk through. Be not detained by fear or moved by any altruistic or ethical motives."

---

[61]Any master is not the goal. A master only reflects your need to look beyond to your inner teacher.

Along The Way

The moon as a guide, the earth a path
In between is a playground for me.
Along The Way, nothing lures me to stay
But I'll break for crumpets and tea.

A friendly old soul, we've met before
As lovers, not this time to be.
Still the help you provide, makes me grateful inside
Your embrace is warm, gentle and free.

So is this The Way of the nameless Sage?
To play with whomever you meet?
Take only your staff, you'll find what you need
Along with crumpets and tea.

Nothing In The Way

To realize that everything around you is in transition is to realize that everything around you is nothing. To realize that everything around you is nothing is to realize . . . there is nothing to transcend.[62]

"Master, if there was one thing you could teach the world, what would it be?

"Nothing."

---

[62]As long as you need to "work through," you need to work through "something." However, a dream is a dream is a dream is a dream . . . until you wake from it. You do not transcend the dream that is not real. You awaken to the truth of what "You Are."

Way Beyond Thought

It was a bright sunny day when the master came down from the bluffs of a river. The wind was blowing cool and dry off the water. Just above the shoreline, the master arrived at the spot where a disciple was waiting. The disciple was sitting against a big tree in the sun, listening to the wind rustle intermittently through the branches of a season's spring.

"Do you know why it's sane here?" expressed the master in quiet repose.

"Why?" responded the disciple.

"There are no interrupting thoughts."

The master turned his face to the bluffs and walked on. He was never seen . . . in those parts . . . again.

The End

APPENDIX:
WRITINGS FROM THE MASTER

WHERE EAST MEETS WEST
ONCE AGAIN
TRUE PURPOSE
THE WAY HOME

WHERE EAST MEETS WEST

The dichotomy between Western and Eastern thinking has been used as a nice and neat way to categorize spiritual literature. It is time to take this limitation of thought and wash it away! For we now truly live in a place where East meets West and West meets East. And that is everywhere, as well as *nowhere in particular.* There is no East or West, nor up or down, nor left or right. All categories of thought limit thought itself.[63]

Therefore, salvation is but your release from all concepts.

---

[63]The dualistic thinking you employ to explain your experiences, is actually the cause of those experiences.

Once Again

You acknowledge that I am an old soul? Then give the respect that is due an old soul and listen!

You say there are old souls and young souls, with souls in degrees between. Within the framework of time, this seems true. And those who are older in time are to be respected as teachers of The Way. However, in truth, the concept of time is meaningless.

An old soul looks upon all as one spirit, one mind, and one reality. There is no choice in this matter. For truth is a witness only to the changelessness that you are, while form sees differences, degrees, and choices to be made. Only within the framework of time do differences seem necessary to bring you back to remembering our shared Creation.

It is a fact that reality is shared. The perception is that there seem to be individual perspectives of "separate realities." The world does seem flat from a "limited" view. However, as you gain perspective from an "expansive" point of view, you come to realize that what you thought to be was but a very small and "separate" piece of the picture. Your purpose is revealed from the perspective of the whole, not from your little picture.

A shift in perception encompasses the release from your little corner of the world. This shift occurs when you decide to let go of cherished thoughts that limit your mind's awareness of the greater picture. Then the expansive whole, which has always been, is remembered once again.

True Purpose

When the sage declares "you are more than just a body," many rise up in terror, proclaiming, "Why do you deny the body?"

The sage's statement is not one of denial. It is one of recognizing true purpose.

Those who scramble for words in the name of protecting the "sacredness" of a body/self image are those who fear death. And in the name of this sacredness, they try to protect it. Yet, they mourn the death of it over and over again until they die. This is circular reasoning, and the ego's way of denying the true purpose of the body. Denial out of fear is essential to the ego's survival.

Make the body a sacred item, and it becomes an end unto itself. In itself, the body witnesses to the duality of ever-changing nothingness. Its purpose becomes this: it is born to die. And in between these two "seemingly" relevant events, the body provides opportunities to experience attack and defense, pleasure and pain, giving and receiving.

The first step of acceptance is to realize that you do not determine your body's purpose. When you let go of your preconceived ideas, you will see the body's true role. Now, rather than a witness to your death, it can be seen as a vehicle, a means to your healing, beyond all temporal appearances.

The Way Home

To start the journey involves the conviction that "there is more to living than what my worldview offers." The desire to want to step beyond "this view" is to start your journey home.

As you begin to recognize your time here as a "passing through," you begin to understand the messages of people and events as movement and noise. In the past, many of these messages were interpreted as experiences of pain and frustration. To learn what these conflicts of life events are really about involves a simple willingness for non-defensive honesty. Are you ready?

When you do not allow for any exception, you learn quickly that the conflict you saw acted upon you by another was not about you, it was about them. To protect the body you inhabit may be one thing, but to react with anger or guilt, "as if" the conflict of another acted out on you is about you, is another thing. Honesty demands ownership, but not the ownership of what does not belong to you.

Just like another's actions are not about you, your reactions are not about them; they're about you. Any exception to this breathes life into victim-justification and self-pity. When you allow no exceptions to this rule, you place all battles within your ability to solve them. This is the place that waits for your honest scrutiny because it is only in this place that you free yourself.

When you allow yourself to see your problems as a mirror of your own battle within, you find opportunity to address the source of all your issues. Learn to see your external conflicts as what they are: distractions, so that you can learn to redirect them as a way to explore the dynamics of what is going on inside you. By using your distractions as a means to sensitize yourself to an internal focus, you allow yourself to hear the quiet, calm voice that will guide you to your goal. In calming your mind, you will catch a glimmer of your healing, your way home.

You are not aware of this voice now because you have chosen external distractions to be your guide. These distractions are constant bombardments of unfinished business that keep you locked into a position of looking for security and meaning in a place where it can never be found. That is why a vigorous curriculum of redirection is suggested in the beginning.

The integrity of your freedom to choose for yourself is never violated. Still, the choice you think you have in the world of people, things and events is the delusion that choices you make in the external, ever-changing realm will make a difference for security and meaning.

Therefore, your freedom will seem to be about "choosing between" until you choose to remember the freedom of the Kingdom we all share. By focusing on our true Kingdom instead of this "real world," you might seem to travel far, to a place you never left, but perhaps imagined in your weary dreams.

If you only find rest for an instant out of time, the experience of "remembering" this instant will suffice. As you return to the world of time and place, that quiet moment of rest will be your reminder that you are but a sojourner here. No matter how hard you try to make it work, this place has never been your intended home.

Let your mind be still for just an instant out of time. There is no need of courage or risk here. For who needs those things where the certainty of peace abides?

Take nothing that will distract you along your way
So you will recognize true direction.

Keep no teaching that past learning has brought you
So that "what is" will reveal itself to you.

Cherish no secret judgment about what you
    think you are
So that what You *are* can tell you.

Make no decision about what to do
So you may remember to trust Truth.

Allow no belief to be entertained
So you can see the truth beyond the limits of belief.

Let go of all the nothingness you have grabbed for the sake of security. Your fearful grabbing represents the very thing you try to deny—your death. Look instead at the pain and insecurity your chase has caused you. Let go of your means, your agenda, your way of solving your made-up problems. Your problem still remains . . . only to reappear in a different form.

Though you may encounter troubles along your way, help will always be there for you in a form you least expect. Ask; help will come. You need not be afraid, for I walk before you and have already overcome the world.[64]

the master

---

[64]It is easy to overcome when you realize it is *nothing* that you are asked to overcome.

The master takes a break.